Christmas Angels and Other Tatting Patterns

by Monica Hahn

DOVER PUBLICATIONS, INC., *New York*

"Give HIM the glory"

To my two granddaughters,
Camlyn Marie Gourley
and
Tiffany Danielle Olsen,
who have both taken lessons and
show great promise

Thanks and credit to my family
and friends and Georgia Ann Kumor
for their support and encouragement.

Christmas Angels and Other Tatting Patterns, first published by Dover
Publications, Inc., in 1989, is a revised, corrected and completely reset
republication of two works: *A Christmas Angel & Other Tatting
Patterns,* originally published by Clipper Enterprises, Inc., Duxbury,
Massachusetts in 1982, and *A Christmas Angel & Other Tatting
Patterns—Volume II,* originally published by Monica Hahn, Seattle,
Washington in 1985.

One photograph from *A Christmas Angel & Other Tatting Patterns,*
and one pattern and one photograph from *A Christmas Angel & Other
Tatting Patterns—Volume II,* have been omitted from the Dover
edition. A new Introduction, three completely new patterns and a new
section, "Tatting Instructions," including information from the original books, have been added to this edition. Several items have been
rephotographed for this edition.

Manufactured in the United States of America
Dover Publications, Inc.
31 East 2nd Street
Mineola, N.Y. 11501

Library of Congress Cataloging-in-Publication Data

Hahn, Monica.
Christmas angels and other tatting patterns.

(Dover needlework series)
1. Tatting—Patterns. 2. Christmas decorations.
I. Title. II. Series.
TT840.T38H34   1989   746.43′6041   89-17149
ISBN 0-486-26076-3

Introduction

The origins of tatting are somewhat uncertain and subject to debate; however, from literature and paintings, we know that knotting (an early form of the art) was well known in Europe at least as early as the seventeenth century. As with most forms of needlework, interest in tatting has fluctuated through the years. Today it is enjoying a new high in popularity.

Monica Hahn has been tatting for over seventy years. In that time, she has developed a high level of expertise and displayed considerable talent for design. In this book, she offers patterns for exquisite collars, edgings, medallions and other items, as well as a beautiful collection of Christmas tree ornaments, including two magnificent Christmas angels.

Tatting Instructions

All tatting patterns are made from one basic stitch, the double stitch, enhanced by picots, which are used for decoration or for joining the rings and chains together. Once you have mastered the double stitch, the rest is easy.

Preparing to tat. Thread used for tatting must be uniform, with a very firm twist. Thread made especially for tatting is available, but the fine cotton thread used for crochet also works well. The finer the thread used, the smaller the stitches and the more delicate the tatting. Most of the patterns in this book use size 20, 30 or 50 thread. For practice, use size 10 or 20 thread.

Two different types of tatting shuttles are widely available today. The first type has both ends closed and a removable bobbin. This shuttle is usually made of metal and has a hook or point at one end. The other type consists of an upper and lower piece held together by a post in the center. The center post generally has a hole in it to anchor the thread to. Both ends of this shuttle are open, but the tips should fit together snugly, yet still permit the thread to pass between them easily. Sometimes this type of shuttle has a long point on one end to aid in joining.

While the first type of shuttle is almost always made of metal, the second type can be fashioned from many different materials—wood, silver, ivory, bone, tortoiseshell, abalone, celluloid, horn and plastic, for example. Some antique shuttles are beautifully decorated, monogrammed or engraved.

I prefer to use a metal shuttle with a bobbin because it is

easier to fill. However, sometimes the hook catches the ring thread, jerking the shuttle out of my hand. To solve this, I simply file the hook into a point.

To fill the first type of shuttle, remove the bobbin and wind the thread smoothly around it until it is full. For the second type, insert the end of the thread through the hole in the shuttle and tie. Wind the thread smoothly around the center. Do not allow the thread to project beyond the edges of the shuttle.

The double stitch. Wind a few yards of thread on the shuttle. Hold the shuttle with your right thumb and index finger so that the shuttle is flat, with the thread coming from the back. This thread is called the running line or shuttle thread.

About 12 inches from the shuttle, grasp the thread firmly with the left thumb and index finger. Spread the remaining fingers and wrap the thread over them, bringing it back around to the thumb and index finger *(Fig. 1)*. This circle of thread is called the ring thread.

The double stitch is made in two steps. For the first step, lift the running line with the middle finger of the right hand *(Fig. 2)*. Guide the shuttle under the ring thread, allowing the ring thread to pass between the index finger and the top of the shuttle. Back the shuttle out, allowing the ring thread to pass between the lower side of the shuttle and the thumb. Now the loop you have just made must be transferred immediately from the ring thread to the running line. This is done by shifting the tension from the left hand to the right hand. Although this may seem difficult, it is actually quite

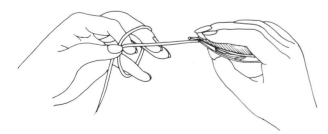

Fig. 1

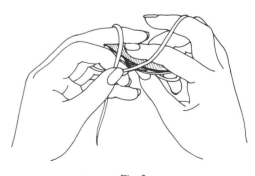

Fig. 2

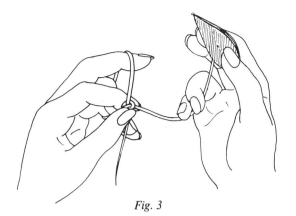

Fig. 3

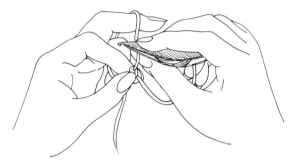

Fig. 4

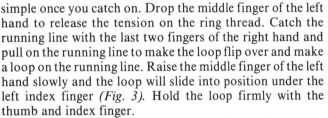

Fig. 5

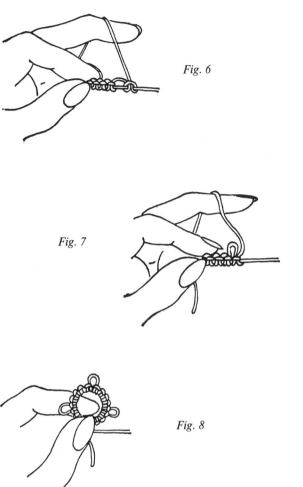

Fig. 6

Fig. 7

Fig. 8

simple once you catch on. Drop the middle finger of the left hand to release the tension on the ring thread. Catch the running line with the last two fingers of the right hand and pull on the running line to make the loop flip over and make a loop on the running line. Raise the middle finger of the left hand slowly and the loop will slide into position under the left index finger *(Fig. 3)*. Hold the loop firmly with the thumb and index finger.

For the second half of the stitch, guide the shuttle over the top of the ring thread *(Fig. 4)*, and back under the ring thread, being sure that the running line hangs free with the thread leading out of the back of the shuttle. Transfer the loop from the ring thread to the running line just as you did for the first half of the stitch, drawing this half close to the first half so there is no extra thread between *(Fig. 5)*. The stitch should slide freely when the running line is pulled away from you. If it does not, the stitch has been locked by a wrong motion and must be taken out. Practice making the double stitch until you can do it easily.

Picots and rings. A picot is made by leaving a space between the stitches. Make 4 double stitches. Make the first half of the next double; slide it on the thread, stopping about 3/16 inch from the last stitch. Complete the double *(Fig. 6)*, drawing the entire stitch close to the stitches already made *(Fig. 7)*. In counting the stitches, the term "picot" refers only to the space between the stitches, not to the double stitch after it. Work 3 more double stitches, another picot, 4 double stitches, another picot and 4 double stitches. Hold the stitches firmly in the left hand and pull gently, but firmly, on the running line until the first and last stitches meet, forming a ring *(Fig. 8)*.

Chains. All tatting designs containing chains and rings are made with one ball and a shuttle (or 2 shuttles). Tie the end of the ball thread to the end of the shuttle thread (or, do not cut the thread from the ball after winding the shuttle). When you are making a ring, use the shuttle thread. When the ring is completed, turn the ring upside down so that the base is

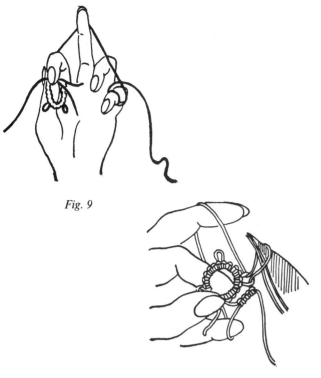

Fig. 9

Fig. 10

held between the thumb and forefinger; place the ball thread over the back of the fingers, winding it several times around the little finger to control the tension *(Fig. 9)*. Work the chain over the ball thread, using the shuttle thread. When the chain is completed, draw the stitches close together. To make the next ring, drop the ball thread and turn the chain so that the base is at the top. With the shuttle thread, make the ring. Picots in chains are made in the same manner as in rings.

Joining. To join rings and chains that face one another, insert the end of the shuttle through the specified picot of the previous ring or chain and pull the ring (or chain) thread through the picot making a loop large enough to insert the shuttle *(Fig. 10)*. A crochet hook may also be used to draw the thread through the picot. Draw the shuttle through the loop and draw the running line tight. This joins the picots and forms the first half of a double stitch. Complete the double stitch. When joining, be sure that all of the shuttle thread is taken in neatly. To test for this, separate the stitches with the right thumb and, if there is a space, take out the excess so it fits neatly. It helps if the running line is kept short.

To join the last ring to the first ring when finishing a motif, work the ring to the join. Hold the ring loosely between the thumb and forefinger of the left hand; fold the lower part under and away from the body, keeping the work between the thumb and forefinger. When the motif is large, sometimes it is easier to pass it under the forefinger, actually wrapping it completely around the forefinger and bringing it back down over the top. Fold the part to be joined toward the knuckle of the finger, being sure that the first ring lines up to meet the last ring so they can be joined easily. Complete the ring and close.

To join chains and rings that do *not* face one another, you must form the loop with the nearer thread or running line. Work the chain to the joining; draw up the stitches to the

required tension (they cannot be adjusted later). Insert the end of the shuttle through the specified picot and draw the *running line* through. Hold the work tightly so that it does not slip and pass the shuttle through the loop. Pull the running line to tighten. Complete the double stitch.

Beginning tatters are often unsure of which thread to join with, the ring or the ball thread. The rule is to always join with the nearer thread.

If you must join additional thread while working a piece, join it at the base of a ring or chain. For a neat join, do not tie a knot; instead, start the ring and weave the short end in and out as you make the d and s for 3 or 4 stitches. If a chain follows the ring, weave the other end into the chain. Clip the ends. This method is very neat and strong. Threads may also be joined with a square knot. Do not cut the ends until the work is finished, since the strain of working may loosen the knot. Never attach a new thread in the ring, as the knots will not pass through the double stitch.

Undoing tatting. Unraveling is possible, but limited. When a mistake is discovered, remove or unwind the thread from the shuttle. This is no problem when making a small motif, but becomes very unwieldy with a large one. Back the thread through the chains and opened rings, using a blunt needle to pull up the thread.

Finishing. Finishing is very important in tatting. Not only does proper finishing make your work more beautiful, it also makes it more durable.

When you reach the end of the pattern, cut the threads, leaving about 2 inches. Tatting stitches are the same on both sides, so decide which side is to be the front of the work and mark it. Using a crochet hook, draw one of the thread ends through the picot, chain or other place where it should be joined; tie the thread ends together in a square knot *(Fig. 11)*. When the entire piece is complete, whip the thread ends to the wrong side of the piece with a fine needle and thread. Sew the ends down for about ¼ inch to ⅜ inch and clip the thread close to the stitching.

If the knot is too big and might show from the right side, simply remove half of the square knot. Spread the knot open and lay one strand on one side of the ring or chain. Sew through the knot and whip down the thread for about ¼ inch; then go back to where you started and lay the other strand in the opposite direction and sew it down. Finish by making a square knot with the sewing thread. Clip all ends.

Sewing the ends to the beginning ring or chain will tend to enlarge it a bit. To compensate for this, omit a double stitch at the beginning and end of the first ring or chain.

Fig. 11

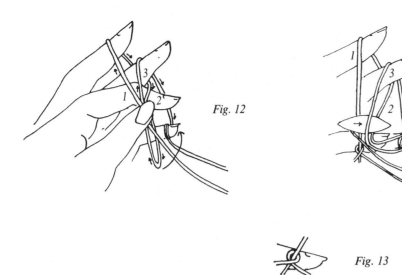

Fig. 12

Fig. 14

Fig. 15

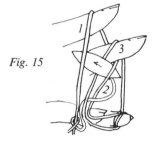

Fig. 13

Block the piece by placing it, right side down, on a padded surface such as an ironing board. Using rustproof pins, pin the piece to the desired shape, measuring carefully to get all of the points even. Place a damp cloth (preferably a linen one) over the tatting and iron the cloth dry. Remove the pins and examine the piece, adjusting the rings and picots if necessary.

If desired, small tatted items such as Christmas tree ornaments can be stiffened with white glue. It is not necessary to sew down the ends if the piece is to be stiffened. Mix 2 teaspoons of glue with 1 teaspoon of water. Place the tatted piece on a white paper towel. Using a small paintbrush, spread the glue solution on both sides of the piece. Dab off the excess glue with a white paper towel. Place a towel on the ironing board, cover it with wax paper. Place the glue-coated piece on the wax paper and pin it to the desired shape. Allow it to dry. Clip the ends.

CLUNY OR PETAL STITCH

The thread on the left hand normally forms the stitches in tatting, but for the Cluny stitch, the shuttle thread is woven back and forth to form the stitches, making a leaf or petal. Begin as you would for a chain. Hold the ball thread firmly between the left thumb and forefinger; pass the thread (1) over the middle and ring fingers, (2) down to the thumb and forefinger; leave a generous loop hanging below the thumb; return the thread (3) over the ring finger and wrap it around the little finger as you would for a chain *(Fig. 12)*. Holding firmly with the thumb and forefinger, pull the loop (be sure it is not twisted) and place it over the little finger. With the shuttle thread, make the first half of the double stitch over thread 1 (the top one) to position the base of the leaf *(Fig. 13)*. Weave the shuttle under thread 3 away from the thumb *(Fig. 14)*, then under 2 and 1 in the opposite direction *(Fig. 15)*. The two movements are considered one stitch. In *Figs. 14* and *15,* the hand has been distorted slightly to show the threads clearly. When actually working the stitch, the thumb will be held over the forefinger, covering the thread. The weaving works better when the shuttle thread is kept short. Be sure the first 2 or 3 stitches are loose, or the thread will not pull freely when the leaf is completed. You may have to push the stitches together with the point of the shuttle as you weave. To form a tip, make the last 2 stitches a little tighter.

To finish the leaf, drop the shuttle and remove the loop from the little finger (be sure that it does not twist). Holding the leaf firmly between the thumb and forefinger, remove the ball thread from the little finger and pull it gently until all the excess thread is gone.

ABBREVIATIONS

ch	chain	rr	reverse ring
cl	close ring	rw	reverse work
d	first half of double stitch	s	second half of double stitch
ds	double stitch	sep	separated
j	join	sp	space
lr	large ring	sr	small ring
p	picot	tw	turn work
r	ring		

Christmas Angels

ANGEL #1

• Size 30 thread. Shuttle and ball.

Body and wings. Wind 2½ yards on shuttle; do not cut thread. Start angel on left breast. R 7 ds, p, 7 ds, p, 7 ds, cl. Repeat r as close as possible to first r; rw. Ch 7 ds, p, 7 ds, p, 7 ds, j to second p of last r, ch 7 ds, p, 7 ds, p, 7 ds; rw. R 7 ds, p, 7 ds, j to same p as last j, 7 ds, cl. R at base of last r, (7 ds, j to p of adjacent r, 7 ds, p, 7 ds, cl) rw. Ch 5 ds, p, 5 ds, p, 5 ds; rw. *R 7 ds, j to free p of last r, 7 ds, p, 7 ds, cl. Repeat r (7 ds, p, 7 ds, p, 7 ds) at base of last r; **rr only.** Ch 7 ds, p, 7 ds, p, 7 ds, j to first p of last r (you will skip nearest p). R 7 ds, p, 7 ds, p, 7 ds, cl; **rr only.** Ch 7 ds, p, 7 ds, p, 7 ds, skip first p and j to next p of last r, ch 7 ds, p, 7 ds, skip first p and j in second p on outside of body. *Start wing* without cutting thread. Ch 6 ds; rw. R 4 ds, p, 3 ds, p, 3 ds, p, 4 ds, cl; rw. Ch 5 ds; rw. R 3 ds, j to last p of last r, 3 ds, p, 3 ds, p, 3 ds, cl; rw. Ch 5 ds; rw. R 3 ds, j to last p of last r, 2 ds, p, 2 ds, p, 3 ds, cl; rw. Ch 5 ds; rw. R 2 ds, j to last p of last r, 2 ds, p, 2 ds, p, 2 ds, cl; rw. Ch 6 ds; rw. R 4 ds, j to last p of last r, 4 ds, cl; rw. Make a r with ball thread of 4 ds, p, 4 ds, cl. Ch 6 ds, j to free p on 4th r of wing, 5 ds; rw. R of 2 ds, p, 2 ds, j to adjacent free p, 2 ds, p, 2 ds, cl; rw. Ch 5 ds; rw. R 3 ds, j to last p of last r, 2 ds, j to next free p, 2 ds, p, 3 ds, cl; rw. Ch 3 ds, p, 3 ds; rw. R 3 ds, j to last p of last r, 3 ds, j to next p, 3 ds, j to p on bodice nearest lower part of wing leaving upper p on that ch free to fasten head to, 3 ds, cl; rw. Ch 5 ds, Cut and tie to free p that head will be connected to.*
To complete body, wind 2 yards on shuttle and j to base of first two rings made. Ch 5 ds, p, 5 ds, p, 5 ds; rw. Repeat from * to * to match other side.

For center skirt fill in. Wind less than a yard on shuttle; do not cut thread. R 3 ds, j to free p on right of 5th r of body, 4 ds, j to other side of dress, 3 ds, cl. Turn work slightly to make next r. Close to base of last r, make r of 4 ds, j to first free p of inside ch on dress, 4 ds, p, 5 ds, p, 4 ds, j to free p on opposite side, 4 ds, cl. Cut and tie.
Lower part of skirt. Wind 2 yards on shuttle; do not cut thread. Attach to first free p at lower edge; ch 8 ds, j to next p on same ch, 7 ds, p, 7 ds; rw.
R 6 ds, p, 6 ds, j to next free p on body, 6 ds, p, 6 ds, cl; rw. Ch 7 ds, p, 7 ds; rw. Repeat between *'s three more times, joining rings. J last ch as other side, 8 ds, j to last free p; rw. Ch 7 ds, p, 7 ds, p, 7 ds, p, 7ds, j to first free p on ch in last row, *ch 9 ds, p, 9 ds, j in p of next ch.* Repeat between *'s three more times. Finish with ch 7 ds, p, 7 ds, p, 7 ds, p, 7 ds, j to side. Cut and tie.
Head. Wind 1½ yards on shuttle; do not cut thread. R 6 ds, j to p at neck of body, 6 ds, j to other p on neck. 6 ds, p, 4 ds, p, continue (4 ds, p) until there are 8 p's; 4 ds, cl; rw. Ch 4 ds; rw. R 2 ds, p, 2 ds, j to first free p on head, 2 ds, p, 2 ds, cl; rw. Ch 5 ds; rw. R 3 ds, p, 2 ds, j to next free p, 2 ds, p, 3 ds, cl; rw. Ch 6 ds; rw. R 3 ds, p, 3 ds, j to next p, 3 ds, p, 3 ds, cl; rw. Repeat last ch and r two more times. R 3 ds, p, 2 ds, j to head, 2 ds, 3 ds, cl; rw. Ch 5 ds; rw. R 2 ds, p, 2 ds, j to head, 2 ds, p, 2 ds, cl; rw. Ch 4 ds, j to last p on head; rw. Ch 3 ds, j to free p on wing, 3 ds, j in base of first r of previous row, ch 7 ds, j, 8 ds, j, 8 ds, j, 8 ds, j, 7 ds, j, 3 ds, j to free p on other wing, 3 ds. Cut and tie.

Dilute one teaspoon white glue and ½ teaspoon water. With small brush, wet angel well with glue. Dab off excess glue with white paper towel. Pin on ironing board and let dry. Protect ironing board with wax paper.

ANGEL #2

• Size 30 thread. Shuttle and ball.

Wind 2 yards on shuttle; do not cut thread. Start at left breast. R 7 ds, p, 7 ds, p, 7 ds, cl. Repeat r as close as possible to first r; rw. Ch 7 ds, p, 7 ds, p, 7 ds, j to second p of last r, ch 7 ds, p, 7 ds, p, 7 ds; rw. R 7 ds, p, 7 ds, j to same p as last j, 7 ds, cl. At base of last r, r 7 ds, j to p of adjacent r, 7 ds, p, 7 ds, cl; rw.

*Ch 5 ds, p, 8 ds; rw. R 4 ds, p, 3 ds, p, 3 ds, p, 4 ds, cl; rw. Ch 5 ds; rw. R 3 ds, j, 3 ds, p, 3 ds, p, 3 ds, cl; rw. Ch 5 ds; rw. R 3 ds, j, 2 ds, p, 2 ds, p, 3 ds, cl; rw. Ch 5 ds; rw. R 2 ds, j, 2 ds, p, 2 ds, p, 2 ds, cl; rw. Ch 5 ds; rw. R 4 ds, j, 4 ds, cl; rw. *Tip of Wing.* With ball thread, r 4 ds, p, 4 ds, cl; rw. With shuttle, ch 6 ds, j to free p, 5 ds; rw. R 2 ds, p, 2 ds, j to opposite r, 2 ds, p, 2 ds, cl; rw. Ch 5 ds; rw. R 3 ds, j, 2 ds, j, 2 ds, p, 3 ds, cl; rw. Ch 3 ds, p, 3 ds; rw. R 3 ds, j, 3 ds, j, 3 ds, j to side of breast, 3 ds, cl; rw. Ch 4 ds. Cut. Tie later.*

For other wing use a little more than a yard on shuttle. Begin by joining between the first two rings; repeat from * to *.

Head. Wind 2 yards on shuttle; do not cut thread. R 6 ds, j to p at neck, 6 ds, j to other p on neck, 6 ds, 8 p sep by 4 ds, 4 ds, cl; rw. Ch 4 ds; rw. R 2 ds, p, 2 ds, j to first free p on head, 2 ds, p, 2 ds, cl; rw. Ch 5 ds; rw. R 3 ds, p, 2 ds, j to next free p, 2 ds, p, 3 ds, cl; rw. Ch 6 ds; rw. R 3 ds, p, 3 ds, j to next p, 3 ds, p, 3 ds, cl; rw. Repeat last ch and r 2 more times. Ch 6 ds; rw. R 3 ds, p, 2 ds, j to head, 2 ds, p, 3 ds, cl; rw. Ch 5 ds; rw. R 2 ds, p, 2 ds, j to head, 2 ds, p, 2 ds, cl; rw. Ch 4 ds, j to last p on head; rw. Ch 3 ds, j to free p on wing, 3 ds, j in base of first r of previous row, ch 7 ds, j in base of next r, (8 ds, j in base of next ring) 4 times, 7 ds, j in base of next r, 3 ds, j to free p on other wing, 3 ds. Cut.

Skirt. Wind 9 yards on shuttle; do not cut thread. J in outer p on wing, ch 2 ds, 5 p sep by 2 ds, 2 ds; rw. *R 6 ds, p, 6 ds, cl, r 8 ds, p, 8 ds, cl; rw. Ch 3 ds, 5 p sep by 2 ds, 3 ds; rw. R 8 ds, j to last r, 8 ds, cl, r 10 ds, p, 10 ds, cl; rw. Ch 3 ds, 5 p sep by 2 ds, 4 ds; rw. R 10 ds, j to last r, 10 ds, cl; rw. (Ch 4 ds, 5 p sep by 2 ds, 4 ds; rw. R 10 ds, j to joining, 10 ds, cl; rw) twice. Ch 4 ds, 5 p sep by 2 ds, 3 ds; rw. R 10 ds, j to joining, 10 ds, cl, r 8 ds, j to joining of 8 ds rings, 8 ds, cl; rw. Ch 3 ds, 5 p sep by 2 ds, 3 ds; rw. R 8 ds, j to same joining, 8 ds, cl; rw. R 6 ds, j to 6 ds ring, 6 ds, cl; rw. Ch 3 ds, 3 p sep by 2 ds, 2 ds; rw. R 6 ds, j to joining, 6 ds, cl.*

Drop shuttle; wind shuttle thread on little finger of left hand and use the ball as a shuttle. This will place work in proper position to j skirt to bodice. The left-hand thread will be joined to the bodice. Ch 2 ds, j in wing where first j is made, 3 ds, j in next free p on breast, 3 ds. With shuttle, r 6 ds, p, 6 ds, cl; rw. Ch 2 ds, p, 2 ds, j to center p of opposite ch, 2 ds, p, 2 ds; rw. Repeat bet *'s once, joining center p's of ch's to center p's of opposite ch's. With ball thread, ch 3 ds, join in free p of breast, 3 ds, j to wing, 2 ds; rw. With shuttle, r 6 ds, p, 6 ds, cl; rw. Ch 2 ds, p, 2 ds, j to center p of opposite ch, 2 ds, p, 2 ds. Repeat bet *'s once more, finish with ch 2 ds, 5 p sep by 2 ds, 3 ds, j to bodice of angel. Cut and tie. Sew ends in and clip, or clip ends and touch with glue.

Simple Christmas Tree

• Size 10 or 20 thread, Coats and Clark's Knit Cro-Sheen or any similar heavy thread. Two shuttles and ball.

R 9 ds, 9 p sep by 3 ds, 9 ds, cl; rw. Ch 9 ds, p, 9 ds; rw. R 7 ds, j to last p of last r, 3 ds, 6 p sep by 3 ds, 7 ds, cl; rw. Ch 7 ds, p, 7 ds; rw. R 6 ds, j to last p of last r, 3 ds, 5 p sep by 3 ds, 6 ds, cl; rw. Ch 5 ds, p, 5 ds; rw. R 5 ds, j to last r, 3 ds, 4 p sep by 3 ds, 5 ds, cl; rw. Ch 4 ds, p, 4 ds; rw. R 4 ds, j to last r, 2 ds, 4 p sep by 2 ds, 4 ds, cl; r 4 ds, j to last r, 3 ds, 3 p sep by 2 ds, 3 ds, p, 4 ds, cl; r 4 ds, j to last r, 2 ds, 4 p sep by 2 ds, 4 ds, cl; rw. Ch 4 ds, j to ch opposite, 4 ds; rw. R 5 ds, j to last r, 3 ds, 4 p sep by 3 ds, 5 ds, cl; rw. Ch 5 ds, j to ch opposite, 5 ds; rw. R 6 ds, j to last r, 3 ds, 5 p sep by 3 ds, 6 ds, cl; rw. Ch 7 ds, j to ch opposite, 7 ds; rw. R 7 ds, j to last r, 3 ds, 6 p sep by 3 ds, 7 ds, cl; rw. Ch 9 ds, p, 9 ds; rw. R 9 ds, j to last r, 3 ds, 8 p sep by 3 ds, 9 ds, cl. Turn work.

Measure about one or two yards off the ball and wind on second shuttle. With second shuttle, make a ch of 7 ds, p, 7 ds, p, 7 ds, j by shuttle thread to base of first r, turn work. With first shuttle, ch 8 ds, j by shuttle thread, ch 3 ds, p, 3 ds; rw. R 4 ds, p, 3 ds, cl; rw. Ch 4 ds, p, 4 ds; rw. R 3 ds, j to last r, 4 ds, cl; rw. Ch 4 ds, p, 4 ds, j by shuttle thread, 8 ds, j to base of last large ring. Cut and tie.

Evergreen Christmas Tree

• Size 30 thread. Shuttle and ball.

Wind 4½ yards on shuttle and do not cut thread.
First half of tree. R 4 ds, 3 p sep by 4 ds, 4 ds, cl; rw. Ch 3 ds, p, 3 ds; rw. R 4 ds, j to last p of last r, 3 ds, p, 3 ds, p, 4 ds, cl; rw. Ch 3 ds, p, 3 ds; rw. R 3 ds, j, 3 ds, p, 3 ds, p, 3 ds, cl; rw. Ch 3 ds, p, 3 ds; rw. R 3 ds, j, 2 ds, p, 2 ds, p, 3 ds, cl; rw. Ch 3 ds, p, 3 ds; rw. R 2 ds, j, 2 ds, p, 2 ds, p, 2 ds, cl; rw. Ch 3 ds, p, 3 ds; rw. R 4 ds, j in last p of last r, 4 ds, cl. Drop shuttle and with ball, make a r of 4 ds, p, 4 ds, cl. Ch 3 ds, p, 2 ds, j in free p, ch 3 ds, p, 2 ds; rw. R 2 ds, p, 2 ds, j, 2 ds, p, 2 ds, cl; rw. Ch 3 ds, p, 3 ds; rw. R 3 ds, j to last ring, 2 ds, j, 2 ds, p, 3 ds, cl; rw. Ch 3 ds, p, 3 ds; rw. R 3 ds, j, 3 ds, j, 3 ds, p, 3 ds, cl; rw. Ch 3 ds, p, 3 ds; rw. R 4 ds, j, 3 ds, j, 3 ds, p, 4 ds, cl; rw. Wind shuttle thread around little finger of left hand and drop shuttle. Pick up ball and make a chain of 3 ds, p, 3 ds; *do not rw.* R 4 ds, p, 3 ds, p, 3 ds, p, 4 ds, cl; rw. Ch 3 ds, j to lower ch, 3 ds; rw. R 3 ds, j, 3 ds, p, 3 ds, p, 3 ds, cl; rw. Ch 3 ds, j, 3 ds; rw. R 3 ds, j, 2 ds, p, 2 ds, p, 3 ds, cl; rw. Ch 3 ds, p, 3 ds; rw. R 2 ds, j, 2 ds, p, 2 ds, p, 2 ds, cl; rw. Ch 3 ds, p, 2 ds. R 3 ds, j, 3 ds, cl. With ball thread, r 3 ds, p, 3 ds, cl. Ch 2 ds, p, 2 ds, j, 2

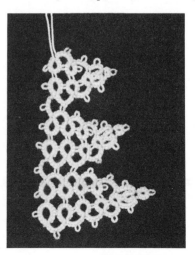

First half of tree.

ds, p, 2 ds; rw. R 2 ds, p, 2 ds, j, 2 ds, p, 2 ds, cl; rw. Ch 3 ds, p, 3 ds; rw. R 3 ds, j to last ring, 2 ds, j to opposite ring, 2 ds, p, 3 ds, cl; rw. Ch 3 ds, p, 3 ds; rw. R 3 ds, j, 3 ds, j, 3 ds, p, 3 ds, cl. With ball thread, ch 3 ds, p, 3 ds. *Starting top tier,* r 3 ds, p, 3 ds, p, 3 ds, p, 3 ds, cl; rw. Ch 3 ds, j to ch on lower tier, 3 ds; rw. R 3 ds, j, 2 ds, p, 2 ds, p, 3 ds, cl; rw. Ch 3 ds, p, 3 ds; rw. R 2 ds, j in last r, 2 ds, p, 2 ds, p, 2 ds, cl; rw. Ch 2 ds, p, 2 ds; rw. R 2 ds, j, 2 ds, cl. With ball, r 2 ds, p, 2 ds, cl. Pick up shuttle again and ch 2 ds, p, 2 ds, j, 2 ds, p, 2 ds; rw. R 2 ds, p, 2 ds, j, 2 ds, p, 2 ds, cl; rw. Ch 3 ds, p, 3 ds; rw. R 3 ds, j, 2 ds, j, 2 ds, p, 3 ds, cl. Cut and tie.

Second half of tree. Fill shuttle with 4½ yards; do not cut thread. Join to base of first r made on first half of tree. Ch 3 ds, p, 3 ds; rw. Repeat the first half of directions through all 3 tiers, joining all rings and chains up the center of the tree. Do not cut, but complete the top.

Top of tree. Ch 2 ds, p, 2 ds, j in base of opposite r; rw. With shuttle, r 3 ds, j to free p on ch left of center, 3 ds, p, 3 ds, p, 3 ds, cl. Large r 3 ds, j, 2 ds, 4 p sep by 2 ds, 3 ds, cl. R 3 ds, j, 3 ds, p, 3 ds, j to free p on ch to right of center, 3 ds, cl. Cut and tie.

Base of tree. With shuttle only, r 3 ds, 3 p sep by 3 ds, 3 ds, cl. Do not make rings too close—leave about ¹/₁₆ inch between each one. R 3 ds, j to last p of last r, 4 ds, j to 5th free p on tree, 4 ds, p, 3 ds, cl. R 3 ds, j to last p on last r, 2 ds, j to tree, 2 ds, p, 3 ds, cl. R 3 ds, j, 4 ds, j to tree, 4 ds, p, 3 ds. R 3 ds, j, 3 ds, p, 3 ds, p, 3 ds, cl. R 3 ds, j, 2 ds, p, 2 ds, j, 3 ds, cl. Cut and tie.

Oriental Christmas Tree

• Size 20 thread. Shuttle and ball.

Wind 2½ yards on shuttle. You may cut and tie a knot to the ball thread to begin a ch *or* place a safety pin on thread to hold as a p so you can j to it later.

First tier. Ch 3 ds, p, 3 ds; rw, small p, 2 ds; rw, 1 ds, 10 p sep by 2 ds, 2 ds; rw, 10 ds, j to small p. Ch 3 ds, p, 4 ds, p, 2 ds; rw, 1 ds, 3 p sep by 2 ds, 2 ds, j to last p of 10 p group, 2 ds, 7 p sep by 2 ds; rw, 10 ds, j to p just before last long series of p's (turning p), 3 ds, p, 4 ds, p; rw, 2 ds, 3 p sep by 2 ds, 2 ds, j in 7th p of last long series of p's (see photo), 2 ds, 7 p sep by 2 ds, 2 ds; rw, 10 ds, j, 3 ds, p, 4 ds, p; rw, 2 ds, 3 p sep by 2 ds, j, 2 ds, 9 p sep by 2 ds, 2 ds, j to turning p by shuttle thread to form ring; rw, 4 ds, p, 3 ds, p, 10 ds, j to 4th p from end of center circle by shuttle thread; rw, 2 ds, 10 p sep by 2 ds, 2 ds, j to turning p (before 10 ch ds); rw, 4 ds, p, 3 ds, p, 10 ds, j as in photo; rw, 2 ds, 10 p sep by 2 ds, 2 ds, j; rw, 4 ds, p, 3 ds, p, 10 ds, j; rw, 2 ds, 10 p sep by 2 ds, 2 ds, j to turning p, 3 ds, p, 3 ds; turn work. R 4 ds, p, 4 ds, j to first free p of last row, 4 ds, p, 4 ds, cl; rw. Ch 4 ds, p, 4 ds; rw. Repeat to end. Join 6 rings together and fasten to p held by pin or knot. Cut and tie.

Second tier. Begin as for first tier. Instead of 10 ds, make only 8 ds and where 10 p are required make only 8. Reduce center circle by 2 p's. J to lower tier as illustrated, to first, center and last ch of previous row. After turning, make ch on end, 3 ds, p, 3 ds, and rings with 3 ds between p. The three little r's on top have 2 ds between p's. Finish with ch 3 ds, p, 3 ds. Cut and tie to base of r.

Hanger. R 3 ds, p, 3 ds, j to top free p, 3 ds, j to last free p, 3 ds, p, 3 ds, cl. Leave a length of thread for hanging, cut and tie.

Base. R 3 ds, 3 p sep by 3 ds, 3 ds, cl. Ch 4 ds, j to tree, 4 ds, j to last p of r, 2 ds, j to center of center r on tree, 2 ds; rw, make p; rw, 4 ds, j to tree, 4 ds. R 3 ds, j to p on ch, 3 ds, j to middle p of first r, 3 ds, p, 3 ds, cl. Ch 4 ds, p, 4 ds, j to free p on second r, 3 ds, p, 3 ds, cl. R 3 ds, j to free p on first r, 4 ds, p, 4 ds. Cut and tie.

Diamond Medallion Cover for Christmas Tree Ball

• Size 30 thread. Shuttle and ball. 2¼-inch glass or satin Christmas tree ball.

Center. Shuttle only. R 4 ds, 3 p sep by 4 ds, 4 ds, cl; rw. *Leave ⅛ inch thread, r 3 ds, p, 3 ds, cl; rw. Leave ⅛ inch thread, r 4 ds, j to first r, 4 ds, p, 4 ds, p, 4 ds, cl; rw. Leave ⅛ inch, r 3 ds, j, 2 ds, p, 1 ds, p, 1 ds, p, 2 ds, p, 3 ds, cl; rw. Leave ⅛ inch, r 4 ds, j, 4 ds, p, 4 ds, p, 4 ds, cl; rw. Leave ⅛ inch, r 3 ds, j, 3 ds, cl; rw. Leave ⅛ inch, r 4 ds, j, 4 ds, p, 4 ds, p, 4 ds, cl; rw.* Repeat between *'s 7 more times, joining the last large ring to the first large ring. Do not cut thread, but carry it up the side of the large ring to the center picot. Leave ⅛ inch thread, r 3 ds, p, 3 ds, cl. Leave ⅛ inch, j to next large ring. Leave ⅛ inch, r 3 ds, j to last r, 2 ds, p, 1 ds, p, 1 ds, p, 2 ds, p, 3 ds, cl. Continue along this side to match the other side of the large rings.

Bottom. Shuttle and ball. R 4 ds, p, 3 ds, p, 3 ds, p, 4 ds, cl; rw. Ch 3 ds, p, 2 ds, p, 2 ds, p, 3 ds; rw. *R 4 ds, j, 3 ds, p, 3 ds, p, 4 ds, cl; rw. Ch 3 ds, p, 2 ds, p, 2 ds, p, 3 ds; rw.* Repeat between *'s until 8 rings and chains are made. Join last ring to first ring. Cut and tie.

To join the bottom to the center, using shuttle only, r 2 ds, j to center p of any ch on bottom circle, 2 ds, cl; rw. Leave ⅝ inch of thread, r 3 ds, j to center p of any large ring on edge of center, 3 ds, cl; rw. *Leave ⅝ inch, r 2 ds, j to center p of next ch of bottom, 2 ds, cl; rw. Leave ⅝ inch, r 3 ds, j to next large r on center, 3 ds, cl; rw.* Repeat between *'s around. Cut and tie to base of first r, leaving ⅝ inch of thread between.

Top. Shuttle only. R 3 ds, j to middle p of any large r on other edge of center, 3 ds, cl; rw. Leave ⅝ inch (this can be adjusted to fit the ball), r 3 ds, 3 p sep by 3 ds, 3 ds, cl; rw. *Leave ⅝ inch, r 3 ds, j to next large r on center, 3 ds, cl; rw. Leave ⅝ inch, r 3 ds, 3 p sep by 3 ds, 3 ds, cl; rw.* Do not join these rings. Repeat between *'s around. Cut and tie to base of first ring, leaving ⅝ inch of thread between.

After finishing, sew all ends in neatly. Lace a length of thread through center picot of free rings. Slip cover over ball; draw free rings up tightly and tie. The extra thread may be slipped into top of ball or touched with glue and clipped.

Round Medallion Cover for Christmas Tree Ball

• Size 30 thread. One shuttle. 2¼-inch glass or satin Christmas tree ball.

Center for medallion. R 1 ds, 12 p sep by 2 ds, cl. Cut and tie. You will need 5 of these.

Next row. Wind 4 yards on shuttle; sr of 2 ds, j to one p on center r, 2 ds, cl; rw. Leave ¼ inch of thread. Lr of 3 ds, 5 p sep by 2 ds, 3 ds, cl; rw. Leave ¼ inch, sr 2 ds, j to next p on center r, 2 ds, cl; rw, ¼ inch thread, r 3 ds, j to last lr, 2 ds, 4 p sep by 2 ds, 3 ds, cl; rw. Continue until 12 sr and 12 lr are made. Make the third (center) p larger on the 5th and 6th rings and on the 11th and 12th rings, so the cover will fit the ball. J last lr to first lr. Cut and tie. The medallion should measure slightly less than 1½ inches in diameter.

Work a second medallion, joining the 11th and 12th lr's to

the 5th and 6th lr's of the last medallion. J 12th lr to first lr. Cut and tie. Continue making the medallions until 5 medallions have been made. On the last medallion, you will have to j 5th and 6th lr's to the last medallion and the 11th and 12th lr's to the first medallion to form a circle. J last lr to the first lr to finish off. Cut and tie. For a larger ball, continue to make and join additional medallions as needed.

Bottom. Lr 1 ds, 10 p sep by 2 ds, cl. Cut and tie. If you have increased the number of medallions, add 2 p for each additional medallion. R 2 ds, j in center p of second free r on any medallion, 2 ds, cl; rw. Leave about ¾ inch of thread (you may have to adjust this to fit the ball), r 2 ds, j to any p on lr of bottom, 2 ds, cl; rw. Leave ¾ inch, 2 ds, j to middle p of next r of same medallion, 2 ds, cl; rw. Leave ¾ inch, r 2 ds, j to next p of bottom r, 2 ds, cl; rw. Leave ¾ inch, r 2 ds, j to center p of next medallion, 2 ds, cl; rw. Continue around in this manner until all medallions have been joined to the bottom ring. Cut and tie the last ring to the first ring, leaving about ¾ inch of thread between them.

Top. Sr 2 ds, j in center p of second free r on any medallion, 2 ds, cl; rw. *Leave about ¾ inch of thread, r 3 ds, 3 p sep by 3 ds, 3 ds, cl; rw. This ring is left free so that it can be gathered with a drawstring to fit the ball. Leave ¾ inch, r 2 ds, j to center p of next ring of same medallion, 2 ds, cl; rw. Leave ¾ inch, make another free ring of 3 ds, 3 p sep by 3 ds, 3 ds, cl; rw. Leave ¾ inch, r 3 ds, j to center p of next ring of medallion, 3 ds, j to center p of first free ring of next medallion, 3 ds, cl; rw. Leave ¾ inch, free ring of 3 ds, 3 p sep by 3 ds, 3 ds, cl; rw. Leave ¾ inch, r 2 ds, j to center p of next r of same medallion, 2 ds, cl; rw.* Repeat between *'s around. Cut thread; tie last ring to first ring, leaving ¾ inch of thread between.

Finish by sewing ends in neatly and clipping, or by clipping and touching ends with glue. Remove the hanger from the ball and place the cover over the ball. Lace a thread through the center p's of the free rings. Draw up the thread and tuck the ends into the top of the ball. Replace the hanger.

To cover a satin ball, tie the ends of the drawstring together and touch the knot with white glue. Clip the ends close to the knot.

Lacy Bell

• Size 30 thread. Shuttle and ball.

Wind 2 yards on shuttle; do not cut thread.

First row. R 4 ds, p, 4 ds, p, 4 ds, p, 4 ds, cl; rw. Ch 3 ds, p, 3 ds; rw. *R 4 ds, j, 4 ds, p, 4 ds, p, 4 ds, cl; rw. Ch 3 ds, p, 3 ds; rw.* Repeat between *'s 4 more times, cut.

Second row. *R 4 ds, p, 4 ds, j to ch of last row, 4 ds, p, 4 ds, cl; rw. Ch 3 ds, p, 3 ds; rw. Repeat from * across, ending with a ring. Cut.

Repeat second row twice more (each row will be one ring shorter). Last row will have 3 rings in it. Be sure to have 2 or 3 yards on the shuttle before starting the 4th row, and do not cut after completing the 3 rings. Ch 2 ds, p, 2 ds, j to side p of last r made, ch 3 ds, p, 4 ds, j to next p on side r, ch 4 ds, p, 4 ds, j to next row, 3 ds, j to p of ch in first row, 5 ds, j to last p on side (on first row). Ch 4 ds, p, 4 ds; rw. Ch 1 ds, p, 1 ds; rw. Ch 3 ds, 11 p sep by 2 ds, 2 ds; rw. Ch 10 ds, j to p made just before the 11-p group, 4 ds, j to free p of r, 4 ds, p; rw. Ch 3 ds, 3 p sep by 2 ds, 1 ds, j to last p of 11-p group, 2 ds, 7 p sep by 2 ds, 1 ds; rw. Ch 10 ds, j to p on opposite ch, 4 ds, j to bell, 4 ds, p; rw. Ch 3 ds, 3 p sep by 2 ds, 1 ds, j to last p of 11-p group, 2 ds, 7 p sep by 2 ds, 2 ds; rw. Ch 10 ds, j, 4 ds, j to bell, 4 ds, p; rw. Ch 3 ds, 3 p sep by 2 ds, 1 ds, j to last p on opposite ch, 2 ds, 3 p sep by 2 ds, 1 ds. With ball thread, make a r of 22 ds for clapper, cl. Ch 2 ds, 7 p sep by 2 ds, 1 ds; rw. J, 3 ds, j to bell, 4 ds, p, 10 ds; rw. Ch 1 ds, j to middle p on side of center ch, 2 ds, 10 p sep by 2 ds, 1 ds; rw. Ch 1 ds, j, 4 ds, j to bell, 4 ds, p, 10 ds; rw. Ch 1 ds, j to 4th p, 2 ds, 10 p sep by 2 ds, 2 ds; rw. P, 1 ds, j to opposite p, 4 ds, j to bell, 4 ds, p, 10 ds; rw. Ch 1 ds, j to 4th p, 2 ds, 10 p sep by 2 ds; rw. Ch 1 ds, j, 1 ds; rw. Ch 4 ds, p, 4 ds, j to side of bell, 5 ds, j, 3 ds, j, 4 ds, p, 4 ds, j, 4 ds, p, 4 ds, j, 2 ds, p, 2 ds, j in base of ring on 4th row, ch 6 ds; rw. R 4 ds, p, 4 ds, j, 4 ds, p, 4 ds, cl; rw. Ch 3 ds, p, 3 ds; rw. R 4 ds, j, 4 ds, j, 4 ds, p, 4 ds, cl; rw. Ch 7 ds, j where pictured. Cut and tie. Stiffen with glue.

Three-Dimensional Bell

• Size 50 thread. Shuttle and ball.

Center ring. R of 1 ds, 8 p sep by 2 ds, cl. Cut and tie.

First row. Wind 2 yards on shuttle; do not cut thread. R 3 ds, p, 3 ds, j to p of center r, 3 ds, p, 3 ds, cl; rw. Ch 6 ds, 3 p sep by 3 ds, 6 ds; rw. R 3 ds, j to last r, 3 ds, j to center r, 3 ds, p, 3 ds, cl; rw. Ch 6 ds, 3 p sep by 3 ds, 6 ds; rw. Repeat r and ch 6 more times. Cut and tie.

Second row. Ch 3 ds, 5 p sep by 3 ds, 3 ds, j to middle p of last row of ch. Continue around. Cut and tie.

Fill shuttle; do not cut thread. R 3 ds, p, 3 ds, j to second p of last ch, 3 ds, p, 3 ds, cl; rw. Ch 4 ds, p, 4 ds; rw. J next r to 4th p of last row. Repeat these r and ch to end of row, then carry the thread to the next level and repeat this row until six or seven rows are made. If it is necessary to increase the ch to make it bell out, by all means do so.

For the clapper, make a string of ds and fasten a bead to it.

Cloverleaf Bell

• Size 20 thread. Shuttle and ball.

Wind 2½ yards on shuttle; do not cut thread.

Middle section. R 3 ds, (p, 3 ds) 3 times, cl; rw. Ch 6 ds, p, 3 ds, p, 3 ds, p, 6 ds, j to third p of r with shuttle thread, 7 ds, 6 p sep by 3 ds, 8 ds; rw. *Start large cloverleaf:* R 5 ds, 4 p sep by 2 ds, 2 ds, j to middle p of first r made, 2 ds, 4 p sep by 2 ds, 5 ds; cl. R 5 ds, j to last p of last r, 2 ds, 12 p sep by 2 ds, 5 ds, cl. R 5 ds, j to last p on last r, 2 ds, 8 p sep by 2 ds, 5 ds, cl; rw. Ch 8 ds, 6 p sep by 3 ds, 7 ds (place small safety pin on shuttle thread here), 6 ds, 3 p sep by 3 ds, 6 ds; rw. R 3 ds, j where safety pin is (removing pin and spreading ch will make joining easier), 3 ds, j to middle p of last big r made, 3 ds, p, 3 ds, cl. Cut and tie.

Top half. Wind 1½ yards on shuttle; do not cut thread. R 6 ds, j to free p of last r, 3 ds, j to next free p of third large r in cloverleaf, 5 ds, p, 4 ds, cl. R 4 ds, j to last r, (4 ds, p) twice, 4 ds, cl; rw. Ch 10 ds; rw. R 3 ds, j to middle of last r, 3 ds, skip 4 p on largest r in center and j to next p, 3 ds, p, 3 ds, cl; rw. Ch 6 ds, p, 5 ds, p, 5 ds; rw. R 3 ds, p, 3 ds, j to last p on last r, 3 ds, j to center p of large r in center, 3 ds, p, 3 ds, p, 3 ds, cl; rw. Ch 5 ds, p, 5 ds, p, 6 ds; rw. R 3 ds, j to 4th p of last r, 3 ds, j to next free p on large r, 3 ds, p, 3 ds, cl; rw. Ch 10; rw. R 4 ds, p, 4 ds, j, 4 ds, p, 4 ds, cl. R 4 ds, j, 5 ds, j, 3 ds, j to first r, 6 ds, cl. Cut and tie.

Open end of bell. Wind 2½ yards on shuttle; do not cut thread. J to middle p of side ch. Ch 6 ds, p, 3 ds; rw. R 3 ds, p, 3 ds, j, 3 ds, p, 3 ds, cl; rw. Ch 3 ds, p, 3 ds; rw. Continue r's and ch's until 10 r's are made, joining third, 4th, 7th, 8th and last r's to bell, ending with ch 3 ds, p, 6 ds. Cut and tie.

Wind 1 yard on shuttle for top hanger. Allow 9 inches of thread, then r 4 ds, p, 4 ds, j to bell, 4 ds, cl; r 4 ds, j to bell, 4 ds, p, 4 ds, cl. Leave about 9 inches of thread; cut and tie. Tie ends of thread together.

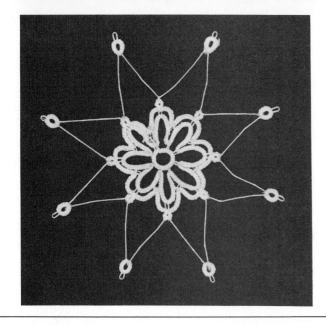

Snowflake Flower

• Size 50 or 30 thread. Shuttle and ball.

Wind a yard or two on shuttle. Do not cut thread.
Center. R 2 ds, 8 p sep by 3 ds, 3 ds, cl; rw. J in last p, *ch 6 ds, 3 p sep by 6 ds, 6 ds, j in center p. Continue around until 8 loops are made. Carry thread to the first free p. Ch 8 ds, j in next p, ch 8, j in next p. Continue around and join in beginning p.
Last row. Wind 2½ yards on shuttle and cut. R 3 ds, j to center loop of last row, 3 ds, cl. Leave ¾ inch thread, r 6 ds, p, 6 ds, cl. Leave ¾ inch thread, r 6 ds, j, 6 ds, cl. Continue until completed.

Daisy Snowflake

• Size 20 thread. Two shuttles and ball.

R 1 ds, 9 p sep by 2 ds, cl. Cut and tie.
Wind 1½ yards of thread on shuttle and, before cutting, measure off 1½ more yards and wind on second shuttle.
First row. First shuttle—r 4 ds, j to any p on center r, 4 ds, cl; rw. Ch 4 ds. Second shuttle—r 1 ds, p, 1 ds, p, 1 ds, p, 1 ds, cl. Ch 4 ds; rw. R 4 ds, j, 4 ds, cl; rw. Continue around, remembering to reverse before and after the r's that j center r's. Cut and tie.
Second row. Wind 1½ yards of thread on one shuttle; do not cut thread. R 1 ds, p, 1 ds, j to center p of r on last row, 1 ds, p, 1 ds, cl; rw. Ch 3 ds, 9 p sep by 2 ds, 3 ds; rw. Repeat r's and ch's around. Cut and tie.

Ten-Pointed Snowflake

• Size 20 thread. Two shuttles and ball.

• d = first half of double stitch.

• s = second half of double stitch.

Center section. Wind 1½ yards on one shuttle; do not cut thread. R 2 ds, p, 2 ds, p, 2 ds, p, 2 ds, cl; rw. Ch 3 ds; rw. R 2 ds, j to last p on last r, 2 ds, p, 2 ds, p, 2 ds, cl. Repeat r's and ch's to form a circle, joining last p to first p in first r. Ten rings in all.
Second row. Measure off 8 yards of thread. Wind 4 yards on one shuttle. Then, starting from the other end of the thread, wind the remaining 4 yards on the second shuttle. R 5 ds, j to any free p on last row, 5 ds, cl. Do not reverse work. Ch 1 ds, (4 d followed by 4 s), repeat this combination until there are 4 sets. 1 ds. (Try for firmness when doing the 4 d and 4 s stitches, as they have a tendency to be loose if done too fast.) Remember to rw only just before r's are made. Tighten the ch of 4 d and 4 s just made and rw. R 3 ds, p, 3 ds, cl. *Do not rw.* Ch one ds, 4 sets of d and s, 1 ds, tighten and rw. R of 5 ds, j to second r of last row, 5 ds, cl; do not rw. Continue around until ten points are made. Tie and sew ends down with fine needle on wrong side.

Small Snowflake

- Size 20 thread. Two shuttles.

Center. R 1 ds, 8 p sep by 2 ds, 1 ds, cl. Cut and tie.
Next row. Measure off 4½ yards of thread. Wind 1½ yards on first shuttle, 3 yards on second shuttle. With first shuttle, r 4 ds, j to any p of center ring, 4 ds, cl; rw. Ch 9 ds. With second shuttle, r 1 ds, 3 p sep by 1 ds, 1 ds, cl. Ch 9 ds; rw. With first shuttle, r 4 ds, j to next free p on center r, 4 ds, cl; rw. Ch 9 ds. With second shuttle, r 1 ds, 3 p sep by 1 ds, 1 ds, cl. Ch 9 ds; rw. Continue around in this manner, remembering to reverse work only before and after the rings that join the center ring. Cut and tie. Sew in ends. Finish by stiffening with glue.

Knobby Snowflake

- Size 20 thread. Shuttle and ball.

Center. With shuttle only, r 2 ds, 8 p sep by 3 ds, cl. Tie and cut.
Second row. Wind 4 yards on shuttle; do not cut. J to any p on center ring, ch 8 ds; rw. (R 6 ds, p, 6 ds, cl) 3 times for cloverleaf; rw. Ch 8 ds, j with ball thread in same p as last ch, tie a half knot to anchor; rw. Ch 3 ds, j with shuttle thread in next free p on center ring; rw. *Ch 8 ds; rw. R 6 ds, j to p of third r of last cloverleaf, 6 ds, cl; complete cloverleaf; rw. Ch 8 ds, j with ball thread in same p as last ch, tie a half knot to anchor, ch 3 ds, j with shuttle thread in next free p on center ring; rw. Repeat until 8 cloverleaves are made, joining last cloverleaf to first one; rw. Ch 8 ds, j in same p as last ch; rw. Ch 3 ds, j at beginning. Cut and tie.
Third row. Wind 2 yards on shuttle. Do not cut. J to a free p on previous row, ch 12 ds. Drop shuttle, measure off 4 yards and wind on a second shuttle. With second shuttle make a r of 4 ds, 5 p sep by 2 ds, 4 ds, cl. Drop shuttle and with first shuttle make a ch of 12 ds, j to next free p on last row, 12 ds, r 4 ds, 5 p sep by 2 ds, 4 ds, cl. Complete row.

Poinsettia

- Two shuttles.
- d = first half of double stitch.
- s = second half of double stitch.

Center. Working with one shuttle only, make a r of 10 p sep by 1 ds, cut and tie.
First row. Wind 2½ yards on one shuttle only. Sr (small ring) 3 ds, j to p on center, 3 ds, cl; rw. Lr (large ring) 4 ds, 3 p sep by 4 ds, 4 ds, cl; rw. Sr 3 ds, j to next free p, 3 ds, cl; rw. Lr 4 ds, j to last lr, 4 ds, p, 4 ds, p, 4 ds, cl. Continue until all 10 p are used. Be sure to j last lr to first lr.
Second row. Take 8 or 9 yards of thread and wind half on each shuttle. If you remember to reverse work (rw) only before each r is made, you will have no trouble. R 5 ds, j to free p on lr, 5 ds, cl. Ch 1 ds, (4 d, 4 s) 5 times, 1 ds; rw. With second shuttle, r 5 ds, p, 5 ds, cl. Ch 1 ds, (4 d, 4 s) 5 times, 1 ds; rw. R 5 ds, j to next free p on center r, 5 ds, cl. Continue around until finished.

Star of Leaves

• Size 30 or 40 thread. One shuttle.

Center. Wind 2 yards on shuttle. R of 5 ds, 11 p sep by 2 ds, 5 ds, cl. R 5 ds, j to last p on previous r, 2 ds, 10 p sep by 2 ds, 5 ds, cl. Continue until 5 r's are made, joining 5th r to first to form a r. Cut and tie.

Leaves. Wind 10 yards on shuttle. R 12 ds, p, 4 ds, p, 5 ds, p, 10 ds, cl; rw. R 12 ds, p, 4 ds, p, 5 ds, p, 10 ds, cl. Join firmly to a center p of any petal of last row, anchor firmly. Leave ¼ inch. R 7 ds, j to p in last r, 7 ds, p, 4 ds, p, 7 ds, cl; rw. R 7 ds, j to p on adjacent r, 7 ds, p, 4 ds, p, 7 ds, cl. Anchor firmly around stem. Leave ¼ inch, r 4 ds, j to last leaf, 7 ds, p, 4 ds, p, 6 ds, cl; rw. R 4 ds, j to p on opposite side, 7 ds, p, 4 ds, p, 6 ds, cl and anchor. Leave ¼ inch. R 4 ds, j to last r, 7 ds, p, 7 ds, j to adjacent leaf, 4 ds, cl. Repeat spray of leaves until 5 points are made. Join large r's of spray to first free p in r's. Sew ends.

Five-Pointed Star

• Size 20 or 30 thread. Shuttle and ball.

Wind 1 yard on shuttle. Do not cut thread.
Center. R 5 ds, long p, 5 ds, cl; rw. Ch 5 ds, p, 4 ds, p, 5 ds; rw. R 5 ds, j to long p, 5 ds, cl; rw. Ch 5 ds, p, 4 ds, p, 5 ds; rw. Continue until 5 r's and ch's are made. Cut thread and tie last ch to base of first r.
Second row. Wind 6½ yards on shuttle. Do not cut thread. *R 4 ds, j to second p of any ch on last row, 3 ds, p, 3 ds, p, 4 ds, cl; rw. Ch 3 ds, p, 3 ds; rw. R 3 ds, j to last r, 3 ds, p, 3 ds, p, 3 ds, cl; rw. Ch 3 ds, p, 3 ds; rw. R 3 ds, j to last r, 2 ds, p, 2 ds, p, 3 ds, cl; rw. Ch 3 ds, p, 3 ds; rw. R 2 ds, j to last r, 2 ds, p, 3 ds, cl; rw. Ch 3 ds, p, 3 ds; rw. R 4 ds, j to last r, 4 ds, cl. With ball thread (putting a rubber band around the ball will make it easier to work with) r 4 ds, p, 4 ds, cl. Ch 3 ds, p, 3 ds; rw. R 3 ds, j to opposite r, 2 ds, p, 2 ds, cl; rw. Ch 3 ds, p, 3 ds; rw. R 3 ds, j to last r, 2 ds, j to opposite r, 2 ds, p, 3 ds, cl; rw. Ch 3 ds, p, 3 ds; rw. R 3 ds, j to last r, 3 ds, j to opposite r, 3 ds, p, 3 ds, cl; rw. Ch 3 ds, p, 3 ds; rw. R 4 ds, j to last r, 3 ds, p, 3 ds, j to next p on next ch of center, 4 ds, cl, ch 2 ds.* Repeat from * to * until all 5 points are made. Sew in ends and stiffen with diluted glue. Finish off with a length of thread for hanger.

Wheel of Nine Rings

• Size 30 thread. Shuttle and ball.

Fill shuttle; do not cut thread. R 8 ds, 3 p sep by 2 ds, 8 ds, cl. A second r of 15 ds, p, 15 ds, cl; rw. Ch 8 ds, p, 9 ds, j in p of last r. *R 10 ds, 3 p sep by 6 ds, 10 ds, cl; using a crochet hook, j by shuttle thread in last j to anchor firmly. Ch 9 ds, p, 8 ds, j in base of r. Ch 4 ds, p, 4 ds. R 8 ds, j in p of opposite r, 2 ds, p, 2 ds, p, 8 ds, cl. Next r, 15 ds, p, 15 ds, cl; rw. Ch 8 ds, j to opposite p, 9 ds, j in p of last r.* Repeat between *'s until 9 rings are made on the outside, being sure to j last segment to first one.

Rose Ornament

• Size 20 thread. Shuttle and ball.

Wind 1½ yards on shuttle. Do not cut thread. R 3 ds, 5 p sep by 3 ds, 3 ds, cl; rw. Ch, small p, 4 ds, j in next p, continue around to beginning. For the next 3 rounds increase the number of ds in each ch of the round to 5, 7, and 9. Don't forget to make small p at beginning of each ch. Omit it on the last row: ch 2 ds, 5 p sep by 2 ds, 2 ds, j in small p, continue around. Cut and tie.

Last round. Wind 5 yards on shuttle. R 5 ds, p, 4 ds, j to second p of last ch on rose, 4 ds, p, 5 ds, cl; rw. Ch 3 ds, 3 p sep by 3 ds, 3 ds; rw. You may have to make the side p of r a little longer than the other p. R 5 ds, j, 4 ds, j to 4th p on rose, 4 ds, p, 5 ds, cl; rw. Repeat around, joining rings to second and 4th p of each ch on rose. Join last ring to first ring. Cut and tie.

Spiderweb Ornament

• Size 30 thread. Two shuttles and ball.

• d = first half of double stitch.

• s = second half of double stitch.

Wind one yard on shuttle; do not cut thread. R 3 ds, 5 p sep by 3 ds, 3 ds, cl; rw. Ch, make a small p, 5 ds, j with shuttle thread in next free p on r, *small p, 5 ds, j with shuttle thread in next free p on ring.* Repeat between *'s around, joining last ch to first small p of round—there will be 6 ch's.

Next round. *Small p, 7 ds, j in next free p on ring.* Repeat between *'s around, joining last ch to first small p of round. Work next 3 rounds in the same manner, increasing the number of stitches between p's by 2 on each rnd—7, 11, and 13.

Next round. *Small p, ch 4 ds, p, 4 ds, p, 4 ds, p, 4 ds, j in joining. Repeat from * around; cut and tie.

Last row. Wind 5 yards on first shuttle and 1 yard on second shuttle. It is important to remember to do all the rings with shuttle #1. For ch, wrap #1 shuttle thread around little finger of left hand and work with shuttle #2. This will make the points lie flat. R 3 ds, j to joining as pictured, 3 ds, cl. Drop shuttle #1 and wind this thread around little finger of left hand and work ch with shuttle #2. Ch 1 ds, work (4 d, 4 s) 5 times, 1 ds. With first shuttle, r 4 ds, p, 4 ds, cl. Wind first shuttle thread around little finger and repeat last ch. Repeat points until 6 points are made.

Lacy Snowman

• Shuttle and ball.

Head. Wind 1½ yards on shuttle; do not cut thread. R 2 ds, 5 p sep by 2 ds, 2 ds, cl; rw. Ch 2 ds, 5 p sep by 2 ds, 2 ds; rw. Make 8 rings and chains, joining each r by second p to 4th p of last r. Join last r to first r in same manner.

Body. Wind 3 yards on shuttle; do not cut thread. Make body just like head but make 3 ds between picots instead of 2. Make 11 rings and chains instead of 8, joining 11th r to first r. Be sure to j center p of last 2 chains of body to center picots of 2 chains on head.

Webbed-Face Snowman

• d = first half of double stitch.

• s = second half of double stitch.

Head. Shuttle and ball. R 4 ds, p, 2 ds, long p, 2 ds, p, 4 ds, cl; rw. *Ch 8 ds; rw. R 4 ds, j, 2 ds, p, 2 ds, p, 4 ds, cl; rw.* Repeat between *'s until 15 rings are made. Make a very small p in center of ch's 10, 11, and 12 to j body to head.

Body. Shuttle only. R 4 ds, p, 3 ds, p, 3 ds, p, 4 ds, cl; rw. Smaller r, 3 ds, p, 2 ds, p, 2 ds, p, 3 ds, cl; rw. *R 1 ds, j, 3 ds, p, 3 ds, p, 4 ds, cl; rw. Sr 3 ds, j, 2 ds, p, 2 ds, p, 3 ds, cl.* Repeat until 33 r's are made, remembering to j last 3 large rings to small p on head.

Buttons. Shuttle and ball. J to p of center r under neck, ch 4 d, 4 s, 4 d, 4 s, *3 ds, p, 3 ds, wrap shuttle thread around thread where * is, ch 4 d, 4 s, 4 d, 4 s. Repeat until 5 buttons are made. Join to center r on bottom, 2 ds, j to p of next r. Repeat (4 d, 4 s, 4 d, 4 s, j to opposite p) 5 times. Cut and tie.

To fill in center of snowman's face, thread a needle with the thread used for the tatting. Anchor thread at side of face. Insert needle through any p on inside of face. Cross to p opposite; insert needle through it. Cross back and pick up p to right or left of first p, then pick up p opposite. Continue in this way until all p's are connected. End at center of face, anchoring thread by looping it around all of the spokes. Weave around, going under and over spokes alternately. If you have an even number of spokes, your weaving will not come out even. To correct this, go over or under 2 spokes at once at some point in round. Be sure to do this at a different place on each round. When face is completely filled in, weave thread through back of stitches and cut.

Picture Frames

FRAME #1
Approximately 3 inches by 3¼ inches.

• Size 30 thread. Shuttle and ball.

Wind 3 yards on shuttle; do not cut thread. Place a safety pin on thread and begin with a ch. Ch 15 ds, 3 p sep by 3 ds, tw (turn work toward you and continue around until it is upside down—shuttle thread will be coming from the bottom). Ch 3 ds, p, 3 ds, p, 3 ds, remove safety pin and j in hole left by pin, 3 ds, 5 p sep by 3 ds. Tw, *ch 15 ds, j in 9th p from shuttle, 3 ds, p, 3 ds, p, tw, 3 ds, p, 3 ds, p, 3 ds, j to p at start of 15 ds, 3 ds, 5 p sep by 3 ds, tw.* Repeat between *'s until 16 or 17 repeats are completed. Be sure to j the last section to the first one. Do not cut.

Ch 3 ds, 10 p sep by 2 ds, 3 ds, j between sections; repeat around. When completed, tie and leave enough thread for a hanger; cut.

FRAME #2
Approximately 3½ inches by 4 inches.

• Size 50 thread. Shuttle and ball.

First row. Wind 3 yards on shuttle; do not cut thread. R 3 ds, 3 p sep by 4 ds, 3 ds, cl; rw. *(Ch 3 ds, p) 3 times, 3 ds; rw. R 3 ds, j to last p on last r, 4 ds, p, 4 ds, p, 3 ds, cl; rw.* Repeat between *'s until 21 rings are made. End with a ch and fasten to base of first r. Cut and tie.

Second row. Wind 5 yards on shuttle and do not cut thread. J to middle p of first ch made in last row. Ch 3 ds, p, 3 ds, p, 3 ds, j in center p of next ch. Ch 5 ds, p, 5 ds, j in next center p of next ch. *Ch 3 ds, p, 3 ds, p, 3 ds, j, ch 3 ds, p, 3 ds, p, 3 ds, j, ch 5 ds, p, 5 ds, j.* Repeat between *'s 5 more times. Ch 3 ds, p, 3 ds, p, 3 ds, j to beginning of row. Cut and tie or carry to first p of first ch made.

Third row. Ch 2 ds, p, 2 ds, j in next free p, *(ch 5 ds, p) 3 times, 5 ds; rw. R 5 ds, p, 5 ds, j to center p of next ch, 5 ds, p, 5 ds, cl; rw. (Ch 5 ds, p) 3 times, 5 ds, j in next free p, 2 ds, p, 2 ds, j to next p, 3 ds, p, 3 ds, j, 2 ds, p, 2 ds, j.* Repeat between *'s around, ending with ch 2 ds, p, 2 ds, j. Cut and tie.

Last row—Plain edge *(pictured).* J to first p on any 3 p ch to left side of large r. *Ch 5 ds, p, 5 ds, skip one p, ch 5 ds, p, 5 ds, j in next p, 5 ds, p, 5 ds, skip one p, j in next p, ch 3 ds, p, 3 ds; rw. R 3 ds, skip one p, j in next p, 3 ds, cl; rw. Ch 3 ds, p, 3 ds, skip one p, j in next p.* Repeat between *'s until 7 points are made.

Ruffled edge *(not pictured).* J in p to left of large r. *Ch 10 ds, p, 10 ds, j in next free p, (5 ds, p, 5 ds, j in next free p) 8 times.* Then repeat between *'s until 7 points are made. Stiffen with diluted glue and shape ruffled edge.

Tatted Collars

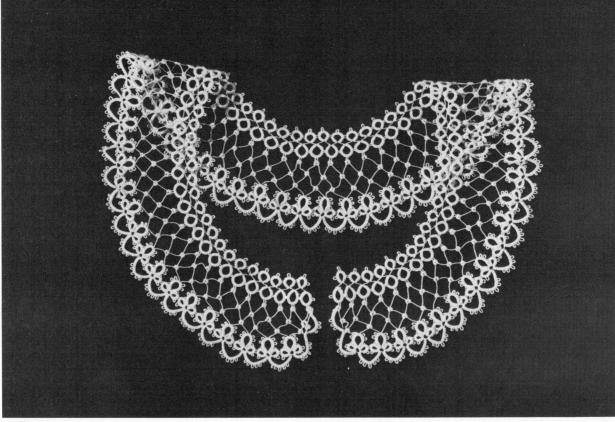

Collar #1

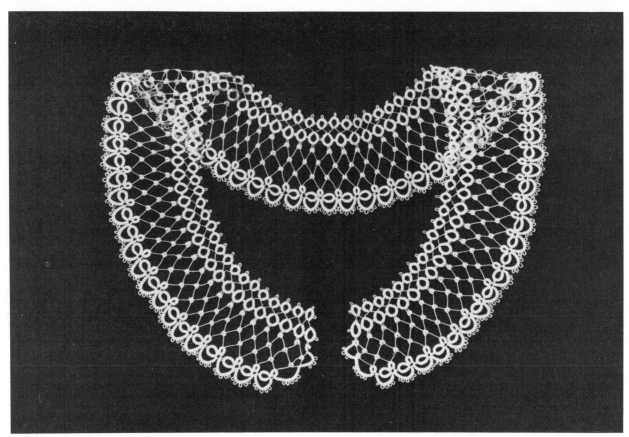

Collar #2

For all collars and cuffs, it is recommended that you use size 30 thread. If you want the collars to be lacier and less stiff, then by all means use a finer thread. I think, however, that these have just enough body and are lacy enough for use with most fabrics.

COLLAR #1

• Shuttle and ball.

First row. Fill shuttle; do not cut thread. When you run out of thread, you can fill from the ball thread at the beginning of the work and work in the opposite direction. Lr 5 ds, 3 p sep by 5 ds, 5 ds, cl. Turn ring upside down—leave ⅛ inch. R 4 ds, 3 p sep by 4 ds, 4 ds, cl. Turn work back to first position. Lr 5 ds, j to first ring, 5 ds, p, 5 ds, p, 5 ds, cl. Turn work—leave ⅛ inch and make r of 4 ds, j, 4 ds, p, 4 ds, p, 4 ds, cl. Continue rings until 70 large and 69 smaller rings are made or until you have the neck size you want.
Second row. R 2 ds, j to middle p of large r on last row, 2 ds, cl, leave ½ inch (measure with a ruler). R of 2 ds, j to second r, 2 ds, cl, ½ inch; repeat to end of row. Turn and make two more rows just like the last one, joining the rings to the ½"-long threads between the rings of the previous row. Cut.
Fifth row. Starting at beginning of second row, j and ch 3 ds, 5 p sep by 2 ds, 3 ds, j between next two rows, ch 5 ds, 5 p sep by 2 ds, 5 ds; rw. Cloverleaf—R 4 ds, 3 p sep by 2 ds, 4 ds, cl, lr 4 ds, j, 2 ds, p, 2 ds, p, 2 ds, j to ½ inch thread in last row, 4 ds, cl, lr 4 ds, j, 2 ds, p, 2 ds, p, 2 ds, j to ½ inch thread in last row, 2 ds, 3 p sep by 2 ds, 4 ds, cl. R 4 ds, j to last p on large r, 2 ds, p, 2 ds, p, 4 ds, cl; rw. Ch 5 ds, 5 p sep by 2 ds, 5 ds; rw. Repeat cloverleaves, joining middle p of first r to middle p of last r in last cloverleaf. Make cuffs in same way, starting with proper number of rings to fit around wrist (I've used 25 small rings and 26 large rings).

COLLAR #2

• Shuttle and ball.

Make first four rows as for Collar #1.
Fifth row. Fill shuttle and j to second row on side of collar (first row of webbing). Ch 5 ds, 3 p or 5 p sep by 2 ds, 5 ds, j to next row on side. Ch 5 ds, 5 p sep by 2 ds, 5 ds. *Do not* j; rw. R 5 ds, j to first loop on last row, 5 ds, cl. R 10 ds, p, 10 ds, cl; rw. Ch 5 ds, 5 p sep by 2 ds, 5 ds, j to p on large r. R 5 ds, j to next thread loop, 5 ds, cl. R 10 ds, p, 10 ds, cl. Continue to the end of the row, adding thread as needed. Omit last 10 ds r and work two ch's as at beginning of row. Cut and tie. Sew in ends and clip. Make cuffs in same way, starting with proper number of rings to fit around wrist.

COLLAR #3

• Shuttle and ball.

Make first three rows as for Collar #1, but be sure to start with 60 large rings and 59 small rings to make the edge come out right.
Fourth row. R 5 ds, j to first thread on last row, 5 ds, cl, r 8 ds, p, 8 ds, cl; rw. Ch 5 ds, p, 10 ds, p, 5 ds, j to lr; rw. R 5 ds, j to next ½ inch loop, 5 ds, cl. R 8 ds, p, 8 ds, cl. Continue to end of row, leaving off the last r of 8 ds, p, 8 ds. Cut and tie.
Fifth row. *R 4 ds, p, 4 ds, j to first free p on collar, 4 ds, p, 4 ds, cl; rw. Leave about ⅜ inch thread. R 5 ds, p, 5 ds, cl; rw. R 4 ds, j to last p of first r, 4 ds, j to next free p, 4 ds, p, 4 ds, cl; rw. Leave ⅜ inch. Lr 6 ds, j to small r, 6 p sep by 3 ds, 6 ds, cl; rw. Repeat first r in row; rw. R 5 ds, j, 5 ds, cl.* Repeat between *'s to end of row. For cuffs, start with 24 large rings and 23 small rings. Continue as above.

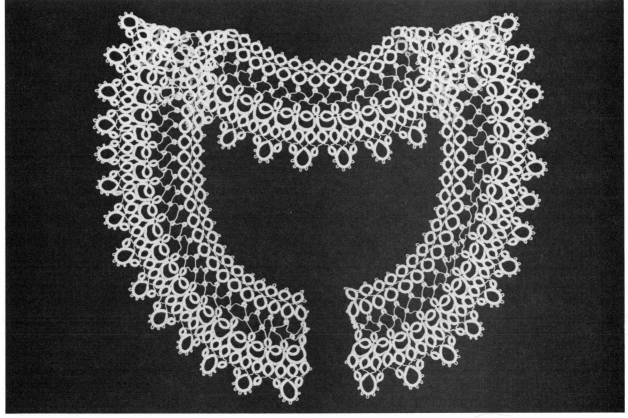

Collar #3

Stationery with Personality

• Glue small tatted "flowers" to stationery and draw in leaves, flowers and other details with colored pencils. Here are 3 different motifs.

• Size 70 thread. This is a good way to use odds and ends of colored thread.

1. Make rings of 1 ds, 9 to 12 long p's separated by 1 ds, cl. Cut. Make several and glue to stationery.

2. White on shuttle and color on ball. Tie together. Make a cloverleaf as follows; r 8 ds, p, 8 ds, cl. Repeat r 2 more times. Tie to base of first r; rw. Ch 9 ds, j to p of r, 9 ds, j to thread between rings. Repeat ch 2 more times, tie and cut. Glue to stationery.

3. R 3 ds, 6 p sep by 3 ds, cl; rw, ch 3 ds, j in next p, ch 9 ds, 2 p sep by 9 ds, 3 ds, 2 p sep by 3 ds, 9 ds, p, 9 ds, j in same p of center r as last joining, ch 3 ds, j in next p, ch 9 ds, j in adjacent p of ch, 9 ds, p, 3 ds, 2 p sep by 3 ds, 9 ds, p, 9 ds, j in same p near center as last joining, 3 ds, j in next p of center r. Continue around center r until 7 large chains are made. Cut and tie. Glue to notepaper.

"Pearl" Necklace

• Shuttle and ball.

String 192 2½-mm beads on ball thread. Then string 192 3-mm beads. Slide them along thread as you fill the shuttle. The shuttle need not be too full to complete both rows. Do not cut thread.

R 4 ds, p, 3 ds, p, 3 ds, p, 4 ds, cl; rw. Pick up clasp. Ch 4 ds, slide 3 beads into place, 4 ds; rw, r 4 ds, j, 3 ds, p, 3 ds, p, 4 ds, cl; rw. Repeat r and ch until 64 points are made. Pick up other half of clasp. Ch 2 ds, j in p on r, 2 ds, j in middle p on r. Then tw upside down and have middle p of rings above the ch you are working on so you can easily j as you work. Ch 3 ds, slide three 2½-mm beads into place, 3 ds, j to next free p on last row. Complete row and turn work right side up and finish with 2 ds, j in side p of last r, 2 ds. Cut and tie to clasp. Sew ends in and touch with white glue to hold.

Earrings

- Use size 70 thread in whatever colors you wish. One shuttle.

Center. R 12 ds, close and cut, leaving two or three inches to tie.

First row. R 12 ds, cl. Repeat 5 times. Close together, cut and tie, leaving two or more inches.

Second row. R 5 ds, 5 p sep by 2 ds, 5 ds, cl. Repeat 5 times, tie to starting end.

Third row. R 6 ds, 7 p, sep by 2 ds, 5 ds, cl. Repeat 6 times.

Cut and tie, arranging last two rows. If desired, this row may be omitted.

Place center inside rings of first row, arranging the rings to form a flower. Pull the loose ends through the center and arrange on the last two rows. Tie securely. Stiffen with glue, and when dry, glue to earring backs. The earring backs can be found in most craft stores.

Napkin Holder #1

- Size 30 and size 60 thread. Shuttle and ball. 1½-inch plastic ring. Crochet hook.

Cover plastic ring with single crochet or buttonhole stitch using size 60 thread. Wind 6 or 7 yards of size 30 thread on shuttle; do not cut thread.

First row. R 3 ds, p, 3 ds, j to plastic ring, 3 ds, p, 3 ds, cl; rw. Ch 3 ds, p, 3 ds; rw. R 3 ds, j to previous r, 3 ds, j to plastic ring, 3 ds, p, 3 ds, cl. Repeat rings and chains until there are 18 rings closely joined together on plastic ring. If the buttonhole stitch is used to cover ring, you may have to use a sewing needle to pierce a hole in the stitches in order to join. (You may use this combination instead of the rings just given: R 4 ds, j to plastic r, 4 ds, cl; rw. Ch 3 ds, p, 3 ds. Repeat until 18 rings are made.) Cut ball thread; carry shuttle thread up side of last ch made and j in p of ch.

Second row. Leave ⅛ inch thread and r 4 ds, p, 3 ds, 3 p sep by 2 ds, 3 ds, p, 4 ds, cl; rw. Leave ⅛ inch thread, r 3 ds, j to next free p on ch of last row, 3 ds, cl; rw. Leave ⅛ inch thread, r 4 ds, j to last big ring, 3 ds, 3 p sep by 2 ds, 3 ds, p, 4 ds, cl; rw. Repeat these rings until all free p are used.

Napkin Holder #2

- Size 30 and size 60 thread. Shuttle and ball. 1½-inch plastic ring. Crochet hook.

Cover plastic ring closely with single crochet using size 60 thread. Fill shuttle with size 30 thread; do not cut.

Join to covered plastic ring, ch 2 ds; rw. Sr 3 ds, p, 3 ds, cl; rw. Ch 3 ds, p, 3 ds; rw. Sr 3 ds, j, 3 ds, cl, r 6 ds, p, 6 ds, cl; rw. Ch 4 ds, p, 4 ds; rw. *R 6 ds, j, 6 ds, cl; rw. Ch 4 ds, 5 p sep by 2 ds, 4 ds; rw. R 6 ds, j, 6 ds, cl; rw. Ch 4 ds, p, 4 ds; rw. R 6 ds, j, 6 ds, cl, sr 3 ds, j, 3 ds, cl; rw. Ch 3 ds, p, 3 ds; rw. Sr 3 ds, j, 3 ds, cl. Drop shuttle and, with ball thread as shuttle, ch 3 ds, j to plastic ring, leaving a little more than ¼ inch, ch 3 ds. Pick up shuttle and make a sr 3 ds, p, 3 ds, cl; rw. Ch 3 ds, j, 3 ds; rw. Sr 3 ds, j, 3 ds, cl, r 6 ds, p, 6 ds, cl; rw. Ch 4 ds, j, 4 ds.* Repeat between *'s 6 or 7 times depending on how big you want the fan to be.

Umbrella Ornament

- This is a lovely favor for a bridal shower.
- Size 20 thread. Shuttle only.

First row. R 3 ds, p, 2 ds, p, 2 ds, p, 2 ds, p, 3 ds, cl. Close to this r make a second r; j first p to last p on first r. Repeat this r until 6 r's are made, j last r to first r made. Cut and tie.

Second row. R 2 ds, j to a free p on last row, 2 ds, cl. Rw, leave ¼ inch thread. R 2 ds, p, 2 ds, cl; rw. R 2 ds, j to next free p, 2 ds, cl. Continue around until 12 small r's are j to first row and 12 small r's are on the outer side.

Third row. Repeat last row, j free p's.

Last row. Wind 8 yds on shuttle. R 3 ds, p, 3 ds, j to free p of small r, 3 ds, p, 3 ds, cl; rw. Leave just a small space. R 3 ds, p, 3 ds, p, 3 ds, p, 3 ds, cl; rw. R 3 ds, j, 3 ds, p, 3 ds, p, 3 ds, cl; rw. Repeat these r's until 24 are made, j every other one to free p of last row. Cut and tie. Stiffen with diluted white glue. When dry, clip ends. Wrap a piece of pipecleaner with white floral tape; glue in place.

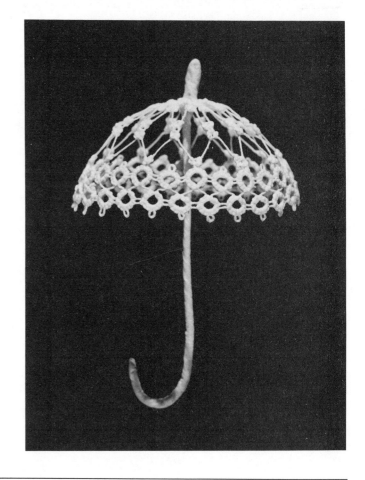

Flat Butterfly

- Size 20 thread. Shuttle and ball.

Center ring. With shuttle only, r 1 ds, 8 p sep by 2 ds, 1 ds, cl. Cut and tie. Wind 3 yards on shuttle; cut thread. R 5 ds, j to center r, 5 ds, cl. Tw and leave about ⅛ inch space. Lr 4 ds, p, 4 ds, 3 p sep by 2 ds, 4 ds, p, 4 ds, cl; rw. Leave space. Sr 3 ds, j to next p of center r, 3 ds, cl. If you examine the illustration you will see that there are 8 lr's, but the 4th and 5th are not joined, and the first and last are free. On the sr's on inside, the first and 5th have 5 ds and the other 6 have only 3 ds. After finishing the 8th sr, tie ends in place where head will be; *make head.* R 5 ds, p, 1 ds, p, 5 ds, cl. Tie and cut.

Outside wing. Wind 1¼ yards on shuttle; do not cut thread. J to side (on head end) in first p of 3 p group in lr. Ch 4 ds, p, 4 ds, p, 4 ds; rw. R 4 ds, j to middle p of same lr, 4 ds, cl; rw. Ch 5 ds, p, 5 ds; rw. R 5 ds, j to middle p of next lr, 5 ds, cl; rw. Ch 5 ds, p, 5 ds, p, 1 ds, j to first p on next lr, 3 ds, j to next p, 4 ds, p, 5 ds, j to middle p of last lr. Small p, 4 ds, j in last p of 3 p group. Tw. Ch 7 ds, p, 7 ds, j to sp made before turning, 4 ds, p, 4 ds, j to next free p, 3 ds, j in next joining, 2 ds, j, 4 ds, p, 4 ds, j, 5 ds, p, 5 ds; tw. R 3 ds, p, 3 ds, j, 3 ds, p, 3 ds, cl; rw. Ch 6 ds, p, 5 ds, p, 5 ds, p, 5 ds; rw. R 2 ds, p, 2 ds, j to next free p, 2 ds, p, 2 ds, cl; rw. Ch 2 ds, j to side p on last r made, 3 ds, j to free p on side, 4 ds, p, 4 ds, j to free p on side of lr, 3 ds. Cut and tie. Repeat for other side.

Antennae. With ball and shuttle, r 6 ds, cl; rw. Ch 22 ds, j in p on head, 1 ds, j in next p, 22 ds; rw, r 6 ds, cl. Cut and tie.

Heart Ring

• Size 20 thread. Shuttle and ball.

Center. R 2 ds, 10 p sep by 3 ds, cl. Cut and tie.

First row. *R 3 ds, j to a p of center, 3 ds, cl; rw. Ch 2 ds, p, 2 ds, p, 2 ds, p, 2 ds*. Repeat from * to * 9 times, cut and tie.

Second row. Fill shuttle. Make heart ring as follows: 9 ds, p, 10 ds, p, 9 ds, j in last p, 10 ds, p, 9 ds, cl. Adjust the V of the heart into the correct position; rw. Ch 7 ds, j in middle p of ch on last row, 7 ds; rw. Heart-ring 9 ds, j to last heart, 10 ds, p, 9 ds, j in last p, 10 ds, p, 9 ds, cl; rw. Repeat ch and heart-ring until row is finished. J last heart to first one made. Cut and tie.

Tatted Butterfly

• Size 30 thread. Shuttle and ball. Crochet hook.

Wind 1½ yards on shuttle; do not cut thread.

First round. R 1 ds, 8 p sep by 2 ds, 1 ds, cl. Ch 2 ds, j in first p.

Second round. *Ch 2 ds, p, 2 ds, j in next p, repeat from * around until 8 loops are made, j last one at base of first complete ch. Ch 2 ds, j in first p.

Third round. *Ch 3 ds, p, 3 ds, j in next p, repeat from * around, j to base of first ch. Ch 3 ds, j in first p.

Fourth round. *Ch 5 ds, p, 5 ds, j in next p, repeat from * around, j to base of first ch. Ch 5 ds, j in first p.

Fifth round. *Ch 4 ds, p, 4 ds, p, 4 ds, j in next p, repeat from * around, j to base of first ch. Cut and tie. Whip ends down with fine thread.

Sixth round. Fill shuttle and do not cut thread. *R 9 ds, 9 p sep by 1 ds, 9 ds, cl (first leaf). Repeat from *, joining first p to last p of last leaf made, until there are 5 leaves. Make base close together. Reverse work. Ch 4 ds, being sure to draw base of 5 leaves close together, p, 4 ds, j to first p of any ch on center, 4 ds, j to next p on same ch, 4 ds, p, 4 ds; rw. R 9 ds, p, 1 ds, p, 1 ds, p, 1 ds, j to 7th p of last leaf made, 6 more p sep by 1 ds, cl. Work 4 more leaves as in first group. Continue around until 8 sets of leaves are made. Cut and tie. Whip ends and clip.

To Form Butterfly. Fold piece in half, matching leaves. Attach a double thread at center of outer edge between scallops, going through both layers. With crochet hook, ch 3, skip 1 ch, slip stitch into next 2 ch, turn work around (not over) and holding the 2 strands under work, slip stitch through both layers in straight line to center fold. *Ch 3, skip 1 ch, slip stitch into next 2 ch, slip stitch into fold, repeat from * once (head and feelers made), turn work and slip stitch back to tail, making same number of sts. Fasten off and whip in ends; trim off.

Finished butterfly.

Cross Bookmark

• Size 70 thread—white and any color. Shuttle and ball.

Wind 6 yards of white on shuttle, tie to colored ball. Begin at corner of first arm. R 6 ds, p, 6 ds, cl; r 6 ds, p, 6 ds, cl; rw. Ch 6 ds, 3 p sep by 2 ds, 6 ds; rw. R 6 ds, j to last r, 6 ds, cl; r 6 ds, p, 6 ds, cl; rw. (Ch 6 ds, 3 p sep by 2 ds, 6 ds; rw. R 6 ds, j to last r, 6 ds, cl; rw) 3 times; do not rw after last r. R 6 ds, j to joining of second and third rings, 6 ds, cl; rw. Ch 6 ds, 3 p sep by 2 ds, 6 ds; rw. R 6 ds, j to last joining, 6 ds, cl; r 6 ds, j to first r made, 6 ds, cl; r 6 ds, p, 6 ds, cl; rw. Ch 6 ds, 3 p sep by 2 ds, 6 ds; rw. R 6 ds, j to last r, 6 ds, cl; r 6 ds, p, 6 ds, cl; rw. (Ch 6 ds, 3 p sep by 2 ds, 6 ds; rw. R 6 ds, j to last r, 6 ds, cl; rw) 3 times; do not rw after last ring. R 6 ds, j to next joining, 6 ds, cl; rw. Ch 6 ds, 3 p sep by 2 ds, 6 ds; rw. R 6 ds, j to same joining, 6 ds, cl; r 6 ds, j to first ring made, 6 ds, cl; r 6 ds, p, 6 ds, cl; rw. Ch 6 ds, 3 p sep by 2 ds, 6 ds; rw. R 6 ds, j to last r, 6 ds, cl; r 6 ds, p, 6 ds, cl; rw. (Ch 6 ds, 3 p sep by 2 ds, 6 ds; rw. R 6 ds, j to last r, 6 ds, cl; rw) 3 times; do not rw after last ring. R 6 ds, j to next joining, 6 ds, cl; rw. Ch 6 ds, 3 p sep by 2 ds, 6 ds; rw. R 6 ds, j to same joining, 6 ds, cl; r 6 ds, j to next joining, 6 ds, cl; r 6 ds, p, 6 ds, cl; rw. (Ch 6 ds, 3 p sep by 2 ds, 6 ds; rw. R 6 ds, j to last r, 6 ds, cl; r 6 ds, p, 6 ds, cl; rw) 4 times. (Ch 6 ds, 3 p sep by 2 ds, 6 ds; rw. R 6 ds, j to last r, 6 ds, cl; rw) 3 times; do not rw after last ring. (R 6 ds, j to next joining, 6 ds, cl; rw. Ch 6 ds, 3 p sep by 2 ds, 6 ds; rw. R 6 ds, j to same joining, 6 ds, cl; rw) 4 times. J at base of first ring made. Cut and tie. Cross measures 10 rings across and 16 rings top to bottom.

To make tassel. Fold a 5-inch piece of cardboard in half and, starting at open end, wind thread around cardboard 20 or 24 times. Tie top threads together and cut other end. Join thread to center chain at top of cross, make a chain of 50 or 60 ds and tie securely to tassel.

Filigree Bookmark

• Size 50 thread. Shuttle and ball.

Sr 3 ds, 3 p sep by 3 ds, 3 ds, cl; rw. Ch 7 ds, p, 7 ds; rw. *Lr 2 ds, j to sr, 2 ds, 6 p sep by 2 ds, 2 ds, cl; rw. Ch 7 ds, p, 7 ds; rw. Sr 3 ds, j to lr, 3 ds, p, 3 ds, p, 3 ds, cl.* Repeat until there are 7 or 8 large rings. Ch 2 ds, sr, 3 ds, j to lr, 3 ds, p, 3 ds, cl; rw. Ch 7, j to last ch, 3 ds, p, 2 ds; rw. R 3 ds, p, 3 ds, j to last sr, 3 ds, p, 3 ds, cl; lr 3 ds, j to sr, 8 p sep by 2 ds, 2 ds, cl; sr 3 ds, j to lr, 3 ds, p, 3 ds, p, 3 ds, cl; rw. Ch 2 ds, j to last ch, 3 ds, p, 7 ds. Sr 3 ds, j to middle p of last sr, 3 ds, p, 3 ds, p, 3 ds, cl. Ch 2 ds. Repeat between *'s down this side, joining all ch's to opposite ch. Work end to correspond with first end. Cut and tie. Sew in ends. Lace ribbon through center.

Bible Bookmark

• Size 50 thread. Shuttle and ball.

Wind shuttle; do not cut thread. *R 7 ds, p, 4 ds, p, 3 ds, cl. R 4 ds, j to last p on last r, 5 ds, p, 5 ds, p, 4 ds, cl. R 3 ds, j to last p on last r, 4 ds, p, 7 ds, cl; rw. Ch 7 ds; rw.* Repeat between *'s 3 more times, joining first p to last one around. Cut and tie. Make 5 squares, joining corners and center. Allow 1 yard of thread for the chains by simply pulling 1 yard off shuttle and begin square. Make two more squares to attach to sides to form a cross. Sew all ends in neatly. Pin on ironing board and, using a wet cloth, iron dry.

To make tassel. Fold a 5-inch piece of cardboard in half and, starting at open end, wind thread around cardboard 20 or 24 times. Tie top threads together and cut other end. Join thread to center ring at top of cross, make a chain of 50 or 60 ds and tie securely to tassel.

Finished water lily.

Water Lily Medallion

• Size 30 thread. Shuttle and *two* ball threads.

Inner ring. Wind a yard of thread on shuttle; cut. R 1 ds, 8 to 12 long (½ inch) p sep by 1 ds, 1 ds, cl. Tie threads securely and cut.

Outer row. Loop thread for second row through picot to avoid a knot. Wind a yard of thread on shuttle; do not cut thread. Ch 3 ds. Add a third thread by holding the end between the fingers, pass thread around hand as usual and wind around little finger. With this thread, ch 3 ds. If these stitches are difficult to hold in place with thumb and index finger, tie the third thread to the picot loop or work the first 3

ds with the 2 chain threads twined together. Turn the 3 ds worked with the second thread downward on the shuttle thread. *Drop this thread (called the lower thread) and, with the first or upper thread, ch 2 ds. Drop the upper thread and, with the lower thread, ch 2 ds, always turning the stitches made with the lower thread downward on the shuttle thread. Use each thread alternately until there are 4 little thread spaces on the upper edge of the cord and 3 spaces on the lower edge. These spaces are formed when the threads are changed. Now, with the upper thread, ch 3 ds, p, 3 ds; with lower thread, ch 2 ds as close as possible for turning point in cord. Continue as before until there are 4 spaces on the upper side and 3 spaces on the lower side, finishing with 3 ds on the upper thread. Join shuttle thread to next picot of inner ring. Ch 3 ds with upper thread to complete the section and make turning. With lower thread, ch 3 ds as close as possible and draw up tightly.* Repeat between *'s around, joining cord to each picot of inner ring. Tie to first picot and cut threads. To make the three-dimensional ornament shown, make 2 medallions and stiffen them with glue. Before the glue dries completely, bend up every other petal on one medallion. Glue this medallion on top of flat medallion; glue a yellow bead to center.

Wind green thread on shuttle. For each leaf cluster, r 5 ds, p, 16 ds, p, 16 ds, p, 5 ds, cl; r 5 ds, j to last r, 24 ds, p, 24 ds, p, 5 ds, cl; r 5 ds, j to last r, 16 ds, p, 16 ds, p, 5 ds, cl. Cut and tie. Glue leaf clusters to bottom of water lily.

This pattern is an original design by Alison Addicks.

Small Flower Medallion

• Size 30 thread. Two shuttles.

Inner ring. Wind less than a yard on shuttle; cut thread. R 2 ds, 11 p sep by 2 ds, 2 ds, cl. Tie threads to form 12th picot. Cut.

Outer row. Wind 1½ yards on first shuttle; without cutting thread from ball, measure off 3 yards and wind on second shuttle. Join shuttle thread to a p of inner ring. Ch 3 ds, p, 2 ds. *With second shuttle, r 1 ds, 7 p sep by 1 ds, 1 ds, cl. Ch 2 ds, p, 3 ds, j to next p of inner ring, ch 3 ds, j to p of previous ch, ch 2 ds.* Repeat between *'s, joining last ch to p of first ch. Tie threads to first p of inner ring. Cut and whipstitch ends.

This pattern is an original design by Alison Addicks.

Rose Pattern

• This attractive rose pattern may be used as an insert on pinafores and other children's clothes, as well as a trim for blouses and shirts.

• Size 50 or size 60 thread. Shuttle and ball.

Rose. The roses are worked separately, then joined. R of 3 ds, 13 p sep by 2 ds, cl; rw. Ch 3 ds, 6 p sep by 2 ds, 3 ds; rw. R 5 ds, skip first p on inner ring, j in next p, 5 ds, cl; rw. *Ch 2 ds, 7 p sep by 2 ds, 2 ds; rw. R 5 ds, skip 1 p on inner r and j in next p, 5 ds, cl; rw.* Repeat between *'s 4 more times. Ch 3 ds, 6 p sep by 2 ds, 3 ds, j where first ch began. Cut and tie, leaving about 2 inches of thread. Make the number of roses needed.

Joining row. J thread in last p of second ch and first p of third ch of a rose (joining them), ch 4, 7 p sep by 2 ds, 4 ds, j in last p of third ch and first p of 4th ch of rose. Ch 4 ds, 9 p sep by 2 ds, 4 ds, j in last p of 4th ch and first p of 5th ch. Ch 4 ds, 7 p sep by 2 ds, 4 ds, j in last p of 5th ch and first p of 6th ch. Ch 10 ds, j in last p of second ch and first p of third ch of next rose, ch 10, double back and j in last rose joining, ch 10, j in second rose where first j was made. Repeat this row until all roses are joined.

This pattern is translated from a German tatting book, *Schiffchenarbeiten Heft II* by Emmy Liebert, published in Leipzig in 1921.

Oval Doily

Finished size: 7¼ inches by 6 inches.

• Size 50 thread (if worked in finer thread, the doily is especially delicate). One shuttle.

The 4 large medallions in the center are worked first.

First row. Make 8 r's close together; each ring, 8 ds, p, 3 ds, 5 p sep by 1 ds, 3 ds, p, 8 ds, cl. J the first p of each r to the last p of the last r. J the last r to the first one made. Cut and tie.

Second row—outside rings. Lr 6 ds, p, 3 ds, 5 p sep by 1 ds, 3 ds, p, 6 ds, cl; rw. Leave a small section of thread. Small r's are joined to the first row as pictured. Sr 2 ds, j, 2 ds, cl. Two sr's are joined to each r in first row. Join the large rings together as pictured. Join the medallions as pictured.

These 4 medallions have 4 smaller stars to fill in the spaces.

Small stars. Make 6 r's close together; each ring, 6 ds, p, 3 ds, 5 p sep by 2 ds, 3 ds, p, 6 ds, cl. J the first p of each r to the last p of the last r, and join to the large medallions as pictured. J the last r to the first one made. The entire piece should lie flat.

Make small rings to fill in the outer edge as pictured: r 2 ds, j, 2 ds, cl; leave a small space on the thread before making the next small ring. Work back and forth until the oval shape is made.

Double row of rings. R 3 ds, p, 3 ds, j to p of center part, 3 ds, p, 3 ds, cl; rw. Leave about ¼ inch of thread, r 3 ds, 5 p sep by 2 ds, 3 ds, cl; rw. Repeat each r alternately, joining each r to the last r on that side. There should be 73 or 74 rings. Join the last 2 rings to the first 2 rings. Carry thread up to center p of first outer ring. Leave ⅜ inch of thread, r 2 ds, j to next r of last row, 2 ds, cl. Continue around. Repeat this row once, joining rings to loops of thread.

Last row. R 2 ds, j to loop on center, 2 ds, cl; rw. Leave less than ¼ inch of thread, r 6 ds, p, 2 ds, p, 4 ds, p, 2 ds, p, 2 ds, p, 4 ds, p, 2 ds, p, 6 ds, cl; rw. *Leave less than ¼ inch, r 2 ds, j to next loop on center, 2 ds, cl; rw. Leave less than ¼ inch, r 6 ds, j to last large r, 2 ds, j, 4 ds, p, 2 ds, p, 2 ds, p, 4 ds, p, 2 ds, p, 6 ds, cl; rw.* Repeat between *'s around. On tight ends of oval, change large rings to 6 ds, p, 2 ds, p, 5 ds, p, 2 ds, p, 2 ds, p, 5 ds, p, 2 ds, p, 6 ds, cl, so that doily will lie flat. Join last large ring to first large ring. Cut and tie. Finish ends by sewing and clipping.

This pattern is translated from a German tatting book, *Schiffchenarbeiten Heft II* by Emmy Liebert, published in Leipzig in 1921.

Edgings

Curved edging with inner row of rings.

MERRY-GO-ROUND EDGING

• A versatile edging. With a slight change this can be a lovely collar or a beautiful border.

• Size 30 or 50 thread. Shuttle and ball.

Curved edging. R 3 ds, 5 p sep by 3 ds, 3 ds, cl; rw. Ch 5 ds, p, 5 ds, p, 5 ds; rw. R 3 ds, 5 p sep by 3 ds, 3 ds, cl; rw. Ch 3 ds, p, 3 ds, j to 4th p of first r, 3 ds, p, 3 ds; rw. *R 3 ds, p, 3 ds, j to 4th p of last r, 3 ds, 3 p sep by 3 ds, 3 ds, cl; rw. Ch 3 ds, p, 3 ds, p, 3 ds, p, 3 ds; rw.* Repeat from * to * until 8 r and ch are made. R 3 ds, p, 3 ds, j, 3 ds, p, 3 ds, j to second p on first r of circle, 3 ds, p, 3 ds, cl; rw. Ch 5 ds, p, 5 ds, p, 5 ds; rw. R 3 ds, p, 3 ds, j to middle p of first ch on circle, 3 ds, 3 p sep by 3 ds, 3 ds, cl; rw. Ch 5 ds, p, 5 ds, p, 5 ds. R 3 ds, 5 p sep by 3 ds, 3 ds, cl; rw. Ch 3 ds, p, 3 ds, j to 4th p of free r between circles, 3 ds, p, 3 ds; rw. Make a second r with 5 p as before and j to first r. Ch 3 ds, p, 3 ds, j to middle p on ch in last circle made. Continue making circles until desired length is obtained.

This can be used as a collar or on a round doily by adding an inner row of rings. R 3 ds, p, 3 ds, j to first p on ch or the 2nd p of a 2-ch grouping. 3 ds, p, 3 ds, cl. Leave a little space between rings. Leave 2 r free on the inner row and j next 2 rings to inside p of ch's between circles.

Straight edging. Change the rings to 4 ds between the 5 picots instead of 2 ds. And increase the two chains between the circles from 2 picots to 3.

Straight edging.

GRAPE EDGING

• Shuttle and ball.

R 4 ds, 3 p sep by 4 ds, 4 ds, cl; rw. *Ch 4 ds, 3 p sep by 4 ds, 4 ds; rw. Large r 10 ds, p, 10 ds, cl; rw. Ch 4 ds, p, 4 ds, j to first r made as in picture, 4 ds; rw. R 4 ds, j in middle p of first r, 4 ds, p, 4 ds, p, 4 ds, cl; rw. Ch 4 ds, j to p of large center r, 4 ds; rw. R 4 ds, j, 4 ds, p, 4 ds, p, 4 ds, cl; rw. Ch 2 ds; rw. R 4 ds, j to last r, 4 ds, p, 4 ds, p, 4 ds, cl. Ch 2 ds. R 4 ds, j, 4 ds, p, 4 ds, p, 4 ds, cl. Ch 4 ds, j to p on large center r, 4 ds; rw. R 4 ds, j, 4 ds, p, 4 ds, p, 4 ds, cl. Ch 4 ds, p, 4 ds, p, 4 ds, j to base of large r, turn but continue ch, ch 4 ds, p, 4 ds, p, 4 ds, p, 4 ds; rw. R 4 ds, j to second p on ch as pictured, 4 ds, j to r as pictured, 4 ds, p, 4 ds, cl; rw. Ch 4 ds, p, 4 ds; rw.* Repeat from * to * for desired length.

CROWN EDGING

• Shuttle and ball.

R 5 ds, 3 p sep by 4 ds, 5 ds, cl. Large r 5 ds, j to last p of last r, 2 ds, 8 p sep by 2 ds, 5 ds, cl. A third r at same base, 5 ds, j to last r, 4 ds, p, 4 ds, p, 5 ds, cl; rw. This completes one cloverleaf. Ch 7 ds, 9 p sep by 2 ds, 7 ds; rw. Repeat cloverleaf and chain for desired length.

LACY EDGING

• Shuttle and ball.

R 4 ds, 3 p sep by 4 ds, 4 ds, cl. At base of this r, make a large r: r 4 ds, j to last r, 2 ds, 7 p sep by 1 ds, 2 ds, p, 4 ds, cl. Make a third r at base to form a cloverleaf, as follows: r 4 ds, j to last p of large r, 4 ds, p, 4 ds, p, 4 ds, cl; rw. *Ch 7 ds, 3 p sep by 1 ds, 7 ds; rw. R 4 ds, p, 4 ds, j to middle p of last r, 4 ds, p, 4 ds, cl. At base, r 4 ds, 3 p sep by 4 ds, 4 ds, cl; rw. Ch 7 ds, 3 p sep by 1 ds, 7 ds; rw. Repeat cloverleaf, joining middle p of first r to middle p of last r made.* Continue design between *'s for desired length.

HAPPY TALK EDGING

• Shuttle and ball.

R 4 ds, 3 p sep by 4 ds, 4 ds, cl; rw. *Ch 4 ds, p, 3 ds, 3 p sep by 1 ds, 3 ds, p, 4 ds; rw. R 4 ds, p, 4 ds, j to middle p of last r, 4 ds, p, 4 ds, cl. At base of last r make another r of 4 ds, 3 p sep by 4 ds, 4 ds, cl; rw*. Repeat design between *'s for desired length.

Square Cluny Motif

• Size 20 thread. Shuttle and ball.

Wind 2 yards on shuttle; do not cut thread. *R 3 ds, p, 3 ds, p, 3 ds, p, 3 ds, cl; rw. Make Cluny leaf *(see page 6)*, weaving back and forth 15 times.* Repeat between *'s 3 more times. Cut and tie to the base of first ring. This completes first square. Begin a second square, joining center p of first r to center p of any ring on first square. You will have to j the r in the opposite direction than expected, or the leaf will not be correctly positioned. Finish the square, joining next r to next r of first square made. Make and join a total of 4 squares as pictured.

Cluny Medallion

• Shuttle and ball.

Center. Wind 1 yard on shuttle; do not cut thread. R 3 ds, p, 3 ds, long p, 3 ds, p, 3 ds, cl; rw. *Ch 5 ds, p, 5 ds, p, 5 ds; rw. R 3 ds, p, 3 ds, j in long p of first r, 3 ds, p, 3 ds, cl; rw.* Repeat between *'s 3 more times. Ch 5 ds, p, 5 ds, p, 5 ds. Fasten in base of first r. Cut and tie.

Next row. Wind 8 yards on shuttle; do not cut thread. J in first p on one ch on center. *Work a Cluny leaf *(see page 6)*,

weaving back and forth 12 to 14 times; rw. R 3 ds, p, 3 ds, p, 3 ds, p, 3 ds, cl; rw. Work Cluny leaf, j in next p of center ch.* Repeat between *'s around, making 10 rings and 20 leaves. Cut and tie.

Last row. Wind 4 yards on shuttle; do not cut thread. R 3 ds, j in center p of one point of last row, 3 ds, cl; rw. Ch 5 ds, p, 5 ds; rw. R 3 ds, j in same p as last r, 3 ds, cl; rw. Ch 2 ds, 5 p sep by 2 ds, 2 ds; rw.* Repeat between *'s around. Cut and tie.